Biblical Thinking for Building Healthy (

 **9Marks Journal**

info@9marks.org | www.9marks.org

Tools like this are provided by the generous investment of donors.
Each gift to 9Marks helps equip church leaders with a biblical vision and practical resources for displaying God's glory to the nations through healthy churches.

Donate at: www.9marks.org/donate.

Or make checks payable to "9Marks" and mail to:
9 Marks
525 A St. NE
Washington, DC 20002

Editorial Director: Jonathan Leeman
Managing Editor: Alex Duke
Layout: Rubner Durais
Cover Design: OpenBox9
Production Manager: Rick Denham & Mary Beth Freeman
9Marks President: Mark Dever

For any gift of $300 ($25/month), you'll receive two new 9Marks books published throughout the year. All donations to 9Marks are tax-deductible.
ISBN: 978-1548216344

CONTENTS

4 — **Editor's Note**
by Jonathan Leeman and Alex Duke

5 — **You Can't Plant a Church If You Don't Know What a Church Is**
by Nathan Knight

7 — **Church Plants Need Pastors, Not Entrepreneurs**
By Matt McCullough

10 — **The Priority of Patience, Prayer, and Preaching in Church Planting**
By Josh Manley

13 — **The Church Planter's Second Priority: Raising Up Leaders**
by Mike McKinley

16 — **Personal Evangelism for the Church Planter and the Church Plant**
J. Mack Stiles

19 — **Church Planters, Make Sure Your People Know You Love Them**
By Steve Jennings

22 — **"The Loneliness of Church Planting"**
by John Starke

25 — **The Blessings and Burdens of A Church Planter's Wife**
Gloria Furman

27 — **Stop Launching Churches! Instead, Covenant Together**
By Nathan Knight

29 — **The Calculated Risks of Church Planting: Sending Your Best Members and Elders**
by Juan Sanchez

32 — **What 9Marks Purists Should Know About Planting?**
By Ed Stetzer

35 Church Planting in the Same Building
by Matthew Spandler-Davison

37 Lessons Learned from Church-Planting by Peaceable Division
By Colin Clark

40 How to Do Ministry When You Don't Have Money
By Brian Davis

43 Church Planting across Ethnic Lines
By Joel Kurz

46 Church Planters, Don't Wait to Put Your Documents in Place
By Joel Kurz

49 Planting Churches for Pleasure, Not for Profit
By Nathan Knight

51 Knowing When to Say When: Reflections from a Failed Church Plant
By Derek D. Bass

53 How to Merge Two Church Cultures
By Dave Russell

55 Church Mergers and Tolerable Irregularities
By Brad Wheeler

58 Anatomy of a Church Merger
by John Folmar

60 What I Learned from Two Failed Church Mergers
By Matthew Cunningham

63 When Two Become One
By Jonathan Rourke

Editor's Note

Jonathan Leeman

Alex Duke

Church mergers and church plants represent good news and bad news. The bad news is that it seems more and more churches are declining and in need of a restart. Church plants represent the good news: we have a bourgeoning supply of young pastors who desire to give themselves to the raising up and shepherding of God's flock. And because we have more prospective pastors than open pulpits, we plant churches. Praise God for this "problem"!

9Marks isn't primarily in the business of offering church planting wisdom. We're not a planting ministry. Nonetheless, we want to think briefly about what our DNA means in this context. Perhaps the most important thing we can say is what Nathan Knight and Matt McCullough say in their articles: a church plant is a church, and a church planter is a pastor.

This Journal considers church planting—its loneliness, its effect on sending churches, its demand for creativity in the midst of financial difficulty. We also offer a few creative ideas about *how* to plant a new church. We won't spoil them, but pay particular attention to articles by Matthew Spandler-Davison and Colin Clark.

Our world needs more healthy churches, which means our world needs more faithful pastors who are planting churches—creating something out of nothing—and merging churches—creating something healthy out of something less-than-healthy. Each discipline comes with a list of attenuating challenges and blessings; each requires an identical dependence on preaching the Word, praying, and sharing the gospel.

There's more to be said, and we hope you'll read on.

You Can't Plant a Church If You Don't Know What a Church Is

Nathan Knight

Thinking about planting a church? What do you think you need? The gospel? Yes. The enabling power of the Spirit? Yes. A sending church? Yes. Others to go with you? Yes. Some money? Yes.

But what about a robust ecclesiology?

Ecclesiology can't be assumed nor should it be considered a distraction to the church planter's "mission." It also can't be a kind of add-on that you insert here and there as you have need. Instead, ecclesiology should inform, instruct, and even excite the mission of planting churches to the glory of God.

In other words: church planter, you need a robust ecclesiology that's in place well before you start trying to plant a church.

A church is more than a gathering of people around a preaching point and singing. There are brightly defined lines that have been given to us by the Lord. These lines mark Christians off from the world so as to picture a better city in which we'll all live for eternity. We must take the time to think through these lines and carefully institute them for the good of our neighbor and the glory of God.

We planted Restoration church here inside the District of Columbia in 2010. Allow me to walk you through four of the questions that were instructive to us as we began our work.

WHAT IS A CHURCH?

It sounds ridiculously simplistic, but answering this question proved to be one of the most helpful things we did.

Was our Bible study a church? Was the gathering of people with music and preaching a church? How did we know we "succeeded" in planting a *church*?

By simply breaking down the word "church" (*ekklessia*) in the Bible we learned that the church was an assembly of "called out" ones.

We also found the classic definition wonderfully practical. This definition requires three things before a gathering of Christians is considered a "church":

- The proper preaching of God's Word (Proclaim the Gospel)
- The proper administration of the ordinances (Portray the Gospel)
- Exercising restorative church discipline (Protect the Gospel)

Armed with that definition and those three descriptions, we knew both our goal and success looked like.

WHO MAKES UP THE CHURCH?

The answer to this question might seem easy except for all those warnings in the Bible of false teachers, professors who don't endure, and those who do things in the name of the Lord but were never actually known by him. Therefore, we knew we needed to be careful about who identified with the church.

Texts like Matthew 16:13–20 and 18:15–20 were wonderfully instructive to us. They helped us see the need to properly define both the gospel message and the possessors of that message by binding and loosing people according to their with gospel doctrine and gospel living.

Because of this, we also spent a lot of time teaching on the gospel and what it looked like to live as a Christian. Only after doing all this did we then begin to welcome those around us into the membership of the church we were prayerfully forming (1 Corinthians 12).

WHO TAKES THE ORDINANCES?

Once the definition of a church and the people who make up the church were clarified, we began to discuss the relationship between the church and the ordinances of baptism (Matt. 28:19–20, Rom. 6:1–4) and the Lord's Supper (Mk. 14:22–25; 1 Cor. 11:17–33).

The ordinances were given to the church as signs or markers of the ambassadors of the kingdom. Therefore, we knew instinctively not to practice them until we'd become a church.

On March 28, 2010 we had a ceremony whereby members covenanted together in accordance to our statement of faith and a church covenant. Another man and I were subsequently installed as elders and only after that did we practice baptism and take the Lord's Supper together.

You can imagine the joy of those 18 people that night as we came together and became a church. The very thing we'd been praying, teaching, and talking about for many months finally became a reality. A church had been planted, and Christ was exalted as yet another gathering of Christians had been marked off from the world through the bright, bold lines of membership, baptism, and the Lord's Supper.

WHAT'S MY JOB AS A PASTOR?

We were installed as pastors because our people had been instructed what to look for in the Pastoral Epistles (1 Tim. 3:1–7, Titus 1:5–9). Once we'd become a church and been officially called as pastors, we took our cues from Acts 6:1–6 and 20:17–35.

These passages told us the bulk of our work was to preach, pray, watch out for wolves, shepherd the flock, watch ourselves, care for our families, and make disciples. Hebrews 13:17 stood prominently in our minds as well: we'll answer to God for how we've led these people.

ECCLESIOLOGY MATTERS

A clear ecclesiology on the front end defined our orientation for church planting. It directed us, encouraged us, and kept us focused on God's plan for his people. The work was hard, and it continues to be. But we've never regretted wielding the sword of God's Word in the difficult work of planting churches.

Ecclesiology is one of God's methodologies for glory. It doesn't slow or deviate from mission. Instead, it fuels the church's mission by marking off God's people from the world. Paul wrote to one local church and told them that they were "lights . . . in the midst of a crooked and twisted generation" (Phil. 2:15).

Church planter, think through these questions now. Don't wait to institute clear convictions after you've gathered a crowd, but carefully put them in place as you go. Explain to those around you what you're or not doing, so they can be informed for the good of their neighbor and the glory of God.

ABOUT THE AUTHOR
Nathan Knight is the pastor of Restoration Church in Washington, D. C.

Church Plants Need Pastors, Not Entrepreneurs

Matt McCullough

When I was first assessed as a church planter I remember people often asked me if I thought of myself as an entrepreneurial type. I believe it was a fair question.

It was fair in part because of my background. Imagine the question asked with eyebrows raised: you think *you're* an entrepreneur? At that point I'd never started anything in my life besides a long sequence of degree programs. My fulltime work had been as a small cog in a large university wheel that didn't need me to keep rolling. Like most grad students, I was all too happy to keep reading and writing and teaching in the narrow lane of my chosen field, talking only to the few people who were already interested or the slightly larger crowd who were assigned to pay attention. Whatever a typical church planter may be, I didn't fit the mold.

But that common question made sense, given my background, because of a common assumption that lies just beneath its surface. I believe we often assume church planting requires more entrepreneurial skills than other pastoral contexts. Is that a fair assumption? Should church planters be entrepreneurs?

IT CAN BE HELPFUL

Of course, the answer to that question depends on what we mean by entrepreneur. The Oxford English Dictionary defines an entrepreneur as a "person who sets up a business or businesses, taking on financial risks in the hope of profit." At Harvard Business School, an entrepreneur is one who pursues "an opportunity beyond resources controlled."

These definitions come from a business context that doesn't map exactly onto a local church context, but you can likely see why we associate church planting and entrepreneurship. Church planters set something up from scratch. They do that where they've identified an important opportunity, some sort of gap in what's already available. And they often have to be comfortable making up for limited resources with their own time, sweat, creativity, and flexibility.

As a church planter, you have to be willing to do whatever needs to be done. You can't rely on a well-oiled machine in which you have a limited role to play, doing only what you're good at while other specialists handle everything else. Because there are no systems in place, you have to be able to plan, to see the big picture, and to recognize what steps to take in what order to reach your goals. You've got to deal with constant context-shifting, and you can't be above the range of menial tasks each day might bring.

BUT IT'S NOT NECESSARY AND IT'S NOT SUFFICIENT

All that said, I'm living proof that new churches can thrive without entrepreneurial pastors. You just have to have the right leaders around you. A plurality of elders is a beautiful thing. None of us is meant to be self-sufficient, and my fellow leaders have filled out the many gaps in my own experience and instincts.

But my personal experience is almost beside the point. Being wired as an entrepreneur is not necessary first and foremost because God doesn't say that it is. An entrepreneurial spirit isn't on any list of biblical qualifications. It can certainly be helpful in a church planting context, but any advantage is prudential, not biblical.

You can lead a church plant and not be an entrepreneur. But you shouldn't lead a church plant if you're not a pastor.

After all, "church plant" is itself a bit of a misnomer. It's a statement about chronology, not ontology. Church plants are churches, and churches don't ultimately need entrepreneurs. They need pastors. They need someone to teach them the Bible. To counsel them toward lives worthy of the gospel. To equip them for their ministry to each other.

Of course, in frontier settings, some people need to go from place to place starting new churches, like Paul did. Maybe that's what God has called you to. But one of Paul's top priorities was securing pastors for the churches he planted (Acts 14:23; Titus 1:5). And in the meantime, both face-to-face and through his letters, he did the work of a pastor himself.

TWO QUESTIONS FOR ENTREPRENEURIAL TYPES

If you're drawn to church planting because of your entrepreneurial itch, because you enjoy the thought of a fresh start with new challenges, you'll be vulnerable to a unique set of dangers. Here are a couple questions you should consider before you take up this work.

Why do you want to plant a church?

Entrepreneurs see opportunities in market gaps. They recognize some unmet need, some untapped demand, and they figure out how to fill the void. For some entrepreneurs, what the gap happens to be is less important than the fact that there's a gap. One writer for Forbes.com says the entrepreneur is driven by "a primordial urge, independent of product, service, industry or market." They're not necessarily more drawn to one product than any other. They just love the opportunity to start something in uncharted space.

But that motive will never be enough in healthy church planting. Instead, you must be driven by a love for local churches and the specific work of leading one. If your primary motive is the thrill of a new venture, you'll probably struggle with the mundane, long-term work your church will need, the sort of work that is the essence of pastoral ministry.

You'll need to give in-depth attention to the details of people's lives. Those people may not show much progress for a long time. They may not submit quickly or easily to your counsel. But this is the work of pastoral ministry in any healthy church. Perseverance over the long term, if God allows, is the path to the greatest fruit in the lives of your people; it's also the path to your deepest joy.

What makes your new church necessary?

I've said that entrepreneurs see opportunities in market gaps. They develop and then offer products that aren't available yet. That's true in church planting, too. But we must be careful how we identify both the gap and the product we want to offer.

The only good reason to plant a church is that a specific geographical area needs more healthy churches than it already has. By "healthy church" I mean a weekly gathering where people hear and respond to God's Word on his terms. I mean a community that brings God glory by the quality of its life together. A culture where each person takes responsibility for the discipleship of others, and where that discipleship equips and mobilizes people for ministry where God has placed them. What healthy churches share, in every time and place, is far more important than any contextual features they don't share.

If the gap you want to fill is more specific than the healthy local church-in-general, if it's about some innovative approach to ministry you bring to the table, then you'll probably be emphasizing things the Bible hasn't prescribed and God hasn't promised to bless. And if your goal is to set your new church apart from the church down the street, then you're going to risk divisiveness.

You may also face another temptation on this front: you may see yourself as the unique product the market is missing, the object of its untapped demand. The Oxford English Dictionary online offers one sub-category to its definition of entrepreneur: "a promoter in the entertainment industry." My sense is this shade of meaning may be there, at least under the surface, when we insist that a church planter must also be an entrepreneur. We may believe that what a church plant needs to be successful is the right frontman, a charismatic personality as the face of the church.

But if you're the product you choose to promote, then you're entering a lose-lose scenario. If you fail, you'll have no one else to blame—and if your church takes off because of you, you'll have built it on something other than biblical community. You will have won glory for yourself, not for God.

Credit for the success of any church plant is a zero-sum game. After all, if we're to be faithful church planters, we must agree with John the Baptist: "He must increase; I must decrease" (John 3:30).

ABOUT THE AUTHOR

Matt McCullough is the pastor of Trinity Church in Nashville, Tennessee.

The Priority of Patience, Prayer, and Preaching in Church Planting

Josh Manley

I pastor an ordinary church in an extraordinary part of the world. My city, Ras Al Khaimah, is in the United Arab Emirates. It's extraordinary because it's situated near the tip of the Arabian Peninsula, and five years ago the ruling Sheikh granted land for an evangelical church building here.

Yet, the church that's been planted here is ordinary. Hopefully, what marks our church is what would mark any faithful church in any part of the world.

So if you've come to this article looking for a new technique or tips on how to develop and strengthen your brand, you'll be disappointed. Because the church is the demonstration of the wisdom of God, we must be careful that our labors to pursue its growth and health don't derive from man's wisdom but God's. God-centered ends are accomplished by God-given means.

Therefore, church planter, before you do anything else, you must prioritize three things: patience, prayer, and preaching.

PATIENCE

Among the many images we find in Scripture for the work of ministry, one common principle is the necessity of patience in the work of the kingdom. Think of the farmer sowing his seed (Mark 4:14; James 5:7).

From the beginning, Christians have always been marked out as a waiting people, as many of our fathers "died in faith, not having received the things promised, but having seen them and greeted them from afar" (Heb. 11:13). We serve the God who sees the end from the beginning, who gets particular glory by taking what seems small and unimpressive to this world and slowly growing it into something astonishing, that which can only be explained by his power (Zech. 4:10; Matt. 13:31–32). Among other things, the drama of redemptive history will definitively prove that God was incredibly patient both with his creatures and in his great work of salvation.

As we think about church planting, we must refuse to move quickly when our God is pleased to move slowly. While it may not fit with the zeitgeist of our culture and times, we trust deep, lasting change that's rooted in the gospel doesn't happen overnight. Yes, our God grants breakthroughs and revivals. But for those moments to be genuine and lasting, they must come on God's terms and by his ways.

Pastoral patience demands we labor by faith, trusting that our God knows how to spread and protect the gospel better than we do. For example, when a pastor friend of mine began laboring in his new church, the congregation wasn't yet ready to receive the Bible's teaching on elders. Rather than rush the church toward where they "needed" to be, he waited patiently—for ten years! He knew it would be wrong to split the church over this issue, so he led by teaching and praying until the church was ready. Now that church is thriving under their leadership and bearing much fruit.

Church planters, prioritize patience.

PRAYER

Charles Spurgeon famously called the church prayer meeting "the powerhouse of the church." If it's good for the church, then surely it's good for the church planter.

Of all the good endeavors the apostles could have given themselves to in the early church—both "when the disciples were increasing in number" and when there was conflict between the Hellenists and Hebrews over the neglect of widows—what did they do? They devoted themselves "to prayer and to the ministry of the word" (Acts 6:1, 4). Prayer was pivotal to the election of the first deacons (Acts 6:6), evangelism (Acts 4:31), Peter's release from prison (Acts 12:5, 12), strength in the midst of suffering and imprisonment (Acts 16:25), the health of the Ephesian church and her leaders (Acts 20:36), and the overall work of God in the advance of the gospel.

If your vision to plant a church doesn't include a commitment to public and private prayer, then your vision needs correcting. When the new and cutting-edge is valued over the wisdom of the ages, we're subtly submitting ourselves human cleverness and therefore diminishing our desperate need to pray for the power of God. If our efforts to plant churches aren't attended to by steady, disciplined, private prayer, then what reason do we have to think our churches will reach beyond our generation and into future ones?

The problem with relying too heavily in church planting on techniques or brands or methods that make sense in one particular cultural moment is that our cultural moment will soon pass and give way to another one. So, if you've planted your church while relying on all the wisdom this current cultural moment can give you, just know it's prone to fade with the passage of the time.

Consider instead how it pleases God to expose the wisdom of this world in its folly (1 Cor. 3:19). Unseen by this world, a steady commitment to prayer is seen by our God who is pleased not only to hear but also to act.

Church planters, prioritize prayer.

PREACHING

As the apostle Paul languished in a Roman prison waiting to be executed by the state, he had to consider carefully what advice he should give to Timothy about the future of the church. Of all the advice he could have given, it might surprise us that he narrowed in on preaching: "Preach the Word; be ready in season and out of season" (2 Tim. 4:2). Paul banked the future of the young, emerging, and even fledgling church on the proclamation of the Word of God.

As you think about church planting, will it be evident that you're wholly dependent on the Word to build the church? The true church is built on the Word of God rightly preached. If that's not what's primarily building your church plant, then you may want to ask if you've really planted a church.

From the beginning to the end, the Scriptures make it clear that God gets particular glory when it's obvious his Word is creating and gathering a people. Giving time and attention to preaching makes clear where the church is centered. And as a congregation sits under the preached Word, it makes a statement that in the midst of a world opposed to God, this Word needs to be heard, and we need to humble ourselves before it. We joyfully and carefully submit ourselves to the revealed Word of God in order to know and make known the revealed God of the Word.

So church planters, prioritize preaching, realizing that as you do, you give yourself to the biblically sure means that God himself has promised to bless in time.

CONCLUSION

For the past four and a half years, I've labored to plant a biblical church in a part of the world that desperately needs a gospel witness. While it's an extraordinary place to plant a church, the work to plant it has been pretty ordinary. While the church must always be reforming, reform runs amok when the revealed wisdom of Scripture has been marginalized to make room for the latest pragmatic wisdom.

So church planters, as you patiently "preach and pray, love and stay," you'll find that your church has been planted on fertile soil that bears up good and lasting fruit.

ABOUT THE AUTHOR

Josh Manley is a Pastor of RAK Evangelical Church in the United Arab Emirates. You can find him on Twitter at @JoshPManley.

The Church Planter's Second Priority: Raising Up Leaders

Mike McKinley

About three weeks into my work as the leader of a church plant/revitalization, I was able to put words to something that had been bugging me. Our group of 15 was made up of some who'd come with me in order to help with the work and others we'd "inherited" from the existing congregation we were trying to revitalize. Some members of the group were happy and joyful servants, others were skeptical that it was going to "work" but willing to give it a try, and still others were distrustful and unhappy.

But the nagging feeling I finally was able to put into words is that as dedicated as some of these people were, my wife and I didn't have anyone else in the church who cared as much as we did.

That's not meant as a criticism of those other people; it's simply the reality of church planting. For a church planter, the work can be close to all-consuming. It combines your religion with your career and your livelihood; the stakes can feel very high, and it's unrealistic to expect many other people to feel as invested as you in the nascent church's viability. I know from my own experience and from talking to other church planters that this realization can heighten feelings of isolation and loneliness.

What I longed for in those early days was others to come alongside me and bear the burden of leadership, responsibility, and care. Now, 12 years later, I no longer feel a sense of being alone in the work. As I write this, I'm in the middle of a sabbatical. In my absence, the church's other elders, staff, and deacons have been leading the congregation quite effectively.

YOU NEED TO RAISE UP LEADERS

So, if you're a church planter, you need to first and foremost focus on preaching the Word, week in and week out. Without that, whatever you're planting, it won't be a church. But after that, you must give yourself to developing and cultivating other leaders. Doing so has an impact that reaches far beyond your own personal need to have others share the burden of caring for the church. Here are three other benefits of developing leaders in your church plant:

1. Developing leaders is important for the health of church members.

The most important way you'll help your church members grow is by preaching the Word of God faithfully week in and week out. But pastoral ministry also involves a lot of one-on-one investment in people's lives, and even the most diligent church planter will have limits on the number of people for whom he can care. By developing other leaders who can teach, disciple, evangelize, counsel, and shepherd the flock, you raise up others who can care for the health of all the church members.

2. Developing leaders is important for the health of the congregation as a whole

Having all of the leadership concentrated in one individual is certainly unhealthy for that person, but it's also unhealthy for a church. A plurality of leadership means a congregation isn't held hostage to decisions that have been made without considering the church planter's biases, weaknesses, and blind spots. When more people are involved in a church's leadership, it's less likely that individual members will become dependent on the gifts and personality of the church planter (who may, after all, not be with them forever) and more likely that they'll be built into the life of the church as a whole.

3. Developing leaders is important for mission.

I don't know about your experience of the space-time continuum, but I've found that I can only be in one place at any given time. And that means there are a lot of places I can't be present to proclaim the gospel and disciple believers. Assuming that the same holds true for you, then you're going to need to invest in other people who can go out to places where you are not.

Planting new churches locally and internationally requires leaders who can initiate and oversee the work. Those leaders must come from somewhere, and so you need to invest in developing them.

Church planters have a million things to do, many of which seem urgent. Investing your time in cultivating new leaders might seem like slow work that doesn't produce immediate and measurable results. But in the long run, it'll help strengthen and expand the scope of your ministry.

HOW TO DO IT

Here are three suggestions for how to find and develop new leaders for your congregation and others:

1. Develop leaders by sharing responsibility.

A lot of church planters are control freaks. I don't know if the nature of the work attracts those kinds of people (because it's easier to direct a church you start than one that you inherit from somebody else) or if it makes those kinds of people (because so much seems beyond your control). But you'll never be able to raise up new leaders if you're not willing to let other people share in the responsibility of teaching, making decisions, and caring for the flock.

Some object that it's dangerous to let unqualified people lead the church, and I agree. I suggest you shouldn't do that. Instead, find people who meet the relevant biblical qualifications (Titus 1:5–9, I Timothy 3:1–13) and give them a chance to lead, even if they do things a bit differently than you.

2. Discover leaders by looking around.

Sometimes, a person's abilities and gifts are obvious and right on the surface. But as I look at the leaders our church has helped to raise up, I'd say a good number of them were people I wouldn't have immediately considered as having "leadership potential." That might be because of personality (maybe they're quiet, introverted, unassuming) or culture (I've learned that leadership sometimes looks different for people from different cultures), but I know I've been guilty of overlooking people who eventually became effective leaders. So, how do you discover these people? Look around your congregation and ask questions like:

- Who is already bearing spiritual fruit in the life of the church?
- To whom do people go for help or counsel?
- Who is already doing the work of serving and caring for others without having been given an office or a title?

3. Develop leaders by training.

This is where the rubber meets the road. Once you're committed to raising up new leaders and you've identified potential candidates, you need to start actually training them. This will look any number of different ways[1]—from one-on-one meetings to large group

---

[1] For one example, you can find the curriculum for the first leadership training course that I did in our church in an appendix to my book *Church Planting if For Wimps*.

classes—but you must begin to intentionally invest in helping to grow the character and competencies that the individual will need for the specific service they render to the body.

ABOUT THE AUTHOR
Mike McKinley is an author and the pastor of Sterling Park Baptist Church in Sterling, Virginia.

Personal Evangelism for the Church Planter and the Church Plant

J. Mack Stiles

Most pastors I know start a church plant with a deep desire to do evangelism. In one sense, what else would you do? Hardly any new pastor sets out to start a church by "sheep stealing." They want a vibrant, cross-focused, Jesus-centered church that hums with gospel witness and is filled with excited new believers.

And they'll get right on it after they figure out how to set up a sound system in a high school gym, and puzzle out where the nursery is going to be held in the hotel, and deal with setting up the web page.

Though most pastors see evangelism as a key to spiritual health for the life of a believer and the life of the church, given the astonishing number of things that must be done for a new church plant—not to mention the internal sinful resistance to evangelism—it's easy to lose our fervor in evangelism. Evangelism, it seems, is always pushing the ball uphill.

If evangelism is to be woven into the fabric of the life of a new church plant and its pastor, it takes some thought and planning.

Here are 10 things I've learned that may help.

1. THE TIME TO START EVANGELISM IN YOUR CHURCH PLANT IS BEFORE YOU EVER START THE CHURCH.

If you've been so immersed in seminary or a support ministry such that you're separated from non-Christians, then you need to think how you can treat evangelism as any other spiritual discipline.

Okay—let me tip my hand, if you've not been engaged in regular evangelism you probably shouldn't be starting a church. Regardless, regularly make attempts to share your faith now before you ever start to plant a church. If you wait until you get around to it, you won't ever get to it at all.

2. TEACH, TEACH, TEACH.

Define the gospel: "The Message from God that leads us to salvation."

Define that message: "God, Man, Christ, Response," or "Creation, Fall, Redemption, Consummation."

Define evangelism: "Teaching (or preaching) the gospel with the aim to persuade."

Define biblical conversion, well, biblically. Check out Michael Lawrence's excellent new book on the topic.

And when evangelism is demonstrated or commanded in the text of Scripture you're preaching through, make sure to highlight that for your congregation.

3. GO FOR LOW HANGING FRUIT.

I once noticed a man who attended church occasionally with his wife. I bumped into him after the service and said, "Tim, I'm curious, where are you in your spiritual life?" "I'm not a believer," he told me. "I really just come to make Gina happy." We talked a bit more. I invited them over for lunch and we talked about spiritual life and the gospel.

Nothing much more happened, but Gina later told me that for all the years he was coming to church, nobody had ever asked him about his spiritual condition. Don't let that happen. Many people who show up in church are surprised when people talk more about sports than spiritual truth, and over time it convinces them they're doing okay. Instead, nail your fear of man to the cross and ask new people about their spiritual life.

The best place for pastors and timid evangelists to do evangelism is with the people who come to church. They're in church, after all!

4. DON'T ASSUME THE GOSPEL.

Assuming the gospel is the quickest route to kill a church in a couple of generations. Recently I was in Portland, Oregon, and I noticed the city was filled with empty church buildings.

But there was once a day when vibrant Christians sacrificed their money and time to build those buildings. What happened? They began assuming the gospel. An assumed gospel leads to a twisted gospel, which leads to a lost gospel. And when the gospel is lost, the life blood of the church is drained out.

Check every sermon with a question: "Could a non-Christian come to faith through what I preached today?"

Check the songs you sing. Are you communicating that people can be close to God regardless of the condition of their heart? We do that when we stir affections with a great tune but sing gospel-less words.

Make sure the truth of the gospel is in congregational prayers and Scripture readings; make sure it's clarified in the sacraments (do you fence the Table?). Have people give testimonies to the church before they're baptized, checking it over with them beforehand to make sure the gospel is clear.

When you do membership interviews, make sure when someone is fuzzy on the gospel that they're really believers. Let people know you love talking about the gospel and will happily make time in your schedule to do that. This selects out those who have genuine interest.

Talk about the gospel often with those who love it; more people than you know are listening in, especially children.

5. LEAD IN EVANGELISM.

I suppose this is obvious, but you need to lead in evangelism. It's not enough just to preach the gospel, though that's of first priority. The congregation will know if you're sharing your faith personally. Of course you're so busy with Christians that it makes your job more difficult. Yes, you have a hard job. But tell your congregation of your desire to share your faith, get them to pray, and tell them of your successes and failures.

6. MAKE SURE THAT EVERYONE IS ON GAME.

You want the whole church to speak of Jesus—not just the pastor. This is why the church should regularly be asked about their evangelistic opportunities. And don't forget: they can help you. Tell your members that, if it would help them, you'd love to talk with their non-Christian friends.

Perhaps you'd find it useful to get my book *Evangelism: How the Whole Church Speaks of Jesus* on why a heathy church is the most important means of evangelism.

Champion evangelists in the congregation. Pray for them corporately, and ask them how it's going. If the congregation knows this a priority to the leadership of the church, then they're more likely to practice it as a priority in their lives.

Of course, you want to talk your people to talk about successful evangelistic opportunities, but don't forget to share stories of failure. Ninety-nine percent of my evangelistic efforts don't go anywhere, but when that happens it's helpful just to know that we're in the battle.

7. BE PRACTICAL, BUT NOT PRAGMATIC OR PROGRAMMATIC.

Just like you, your congregation needs help to share their faith. But don't set up a bunch of evangelistic programs. I often say that programs are to evangelism what sugar is to nutrition. Programs may make you feel like you've done evangelism when you haven't, just as eating sugar may make you feel like you've eaten when you haven't.

Having said that, do help your congregation get in the game with some practical helps. Here's an example: Covenant Hope Church in Dubai had everyone write out five non-Christian friends on a card and had people pray about sharing with the folks on that list. How simple and practical. They had them put it in their purse or wallet and they refer to it regularly. Have them think through the plan: an invitation for coffee, an email with an invite to church, etc. Help your congregation understand that if everyone is sharing their faith it will be much more effective than any church-wide evangelistic program, no matter how large that might be.

8. BE BOLD AND CLEAR WHEN YOU SHARE YOUR FAITH.

I don't mean be offensive and abrasive when you share your faith. I just mean take more risks in evangelism. Be honest; let people know where you're coming from. This may sound a bit strange, but one of the great things about being up front about your desire to talk to people about the gospel is that if you're rebuffed, you've saved a lot of time for them and you.

9. KNOW THE GOSPEL, SPEAK THE GOSPEL, AND LIVE THE GOSPEL.

Know how to say the message of the gospel in clear and unassuming language, and make sure members of the congregation know how to say the gospel in a minute or two in their own words, too.

I've noticed something over the years in my attempts to share my faith: if you don't regularly ponder on, pray about, apply, and speak the gospel, then it will become fuzzy and distant. I think it's the spiritual maxim that what you have will be taken away from you—or, to employ a cliché: use it or lose it.

Help the congregation know how to apply the gospel to their lives in areas of sin and repentance, forgiveness and holiness. Help them see how the gospel is not just what gets us saved, but a well in the center of life that we should draw from daily.

10. USE BOOKS NOT TRACTS.

For giveaways and welcome gifts for visitors, prioritize brief and readable books than tracts. So many people I've known have come to faith though *The Cross Centered Life* by C.J. Mahaney, or *What is the Gospel?* by Greg Gilbert.

Don't be chintzy. Give out books that explain the gospel, and train your members to be willing to go over the books with the seekers who get them.

ABOUT THE AUTHOR

Mack Stiles lives in Dubai with his wife Leeann. He serves as an elder of Redeemer Church of Dubai and as the General Secretary of the IFES (parachurch) movement in the United Arab Emirates.

Church Planters, Make Sure Your People Know You Love Them

Steve Jennings

I once asked a long-time pastor: "What's one piece of advice you would give a first-time pastor about to plant a church?"

His answer? "Before you do anything else, make sure your people know you love them."

WHAT LOVE IS NOT

Sometimes in order to understand what loving our people is, we need to understand what it's not. It's not about always telling them what they want to hear, or being a people pleaser, or even trying to get them to love you in return, whatever it takes.

In fact, loving our people isn't about us at all. Rather, to love your people means to show them how dear they are to you by gently and sacrificially giving of yourself to feed them with the nourishment of the gospel for both their eternal good and God's glory. To follow Paul's analogy from 1 Thessalonians 2, this means seeking their good at your expense, their flourishing above your recognition—like a mother. You love them because they are dear to you, having been placed into your care by God.

AIMING FOR LOVE

So, from day one, I endeavored to make that my aim. More often than not, I failed miserably. But by God's grace, I've also seen some fruit.

In the earliest days of our church plant, striving to make sure I loved my people and that they knew it meant at least four things:

1. Disagreement with unity

My city is diverse, and there aren't a lot of options around for church, which means a wide variety of people come to us. There have been times when people have come and disagreed on a variety of practical and/or tertiary doctrinal points, but they've stayed and listened because they sensed deeply that they were loved.

2. Reception of hard words

When people are confident that they're loved, they're much more prepared to receive rebuke. On the other side, I've also experienced what happens when I've not laid the foundation of love and then confronted sin. The difference is staggering.

3. Cultural barriers transcended

My church is very culturally diverse. Caring for people through simple, consistent sacrifice means that many cultural barriers, such as customs of hospitality and liturgical structures, are in time overcome. We've had people from different countries who had a hard time with things like our music or preaching style, but they stayed because they sensed they were led by shepherds who genuinely cared for them.

4. Understanding for pastoral imperfections

Laying the foundation of love has meant an abundance of patience with my own immaturity and failings as a pastor. And we pastors, as fellow sinners, need lots of that. Our people need a context for understanding our shortcomings. They need to know we're imperfect and trust in Christ as our only hope—just like we exhort them to do.

HOW TO PURSUE LOVE

Again, before we can show our people we love them, we must actually love them. And if we're honest, this can be hard, and it's not always something that comes automatically.

So how do we pursue it? A few ideas:

1. Daily pray for your heart to be filled with love for them and then pray for specific people. Make it a habit of praying each day, "Lord, help me to love you, to love my family, and to love your people more." Have a practice of praying for each one by name, such as praying through your membership directory.
2. Soak in the gospel. First John and Ephesians 5 show us the source of our love for our people: a heart-deep knowledge of the love of God expressed in the death of Christ for us. The fountain of our love for our people must be the gospel. Otherwise, we will be fickle and our love will be aimed at the wrong ends.
3. Spend time with them. Love is cultivated through fellowship. To move from love as an idea to love as a reality, there must be a cultivated relationship.

COMMUNICATING LOVE

Finally how do we communicate love to our people? How do we, before anything else, make sure they know we love them?

1. Show hospitality by spending time with them.

Like Paul and the Thessalonians, it must be clear that we don't just preach to them, but that we're sharing our lives with them as well.

Hospitality both grows and shows our love for them. It's important to set up a schedule of pastoral visits and ask questions that show they're important. It's in this context that the little things matter—remembering birthdays, being aware of burdens and illnesses, showing an appreciation for things they enjoy—much like a mother would for her child.

During these times, share with them truth from Scripture and gentle encouragements and admonitions that relate to their current affairs in life. Or, just listen to them talk. Take note of what's burdening them, what they're rejoicing in, and remember it as you pray for them.

2. Listen well to complaints and criticism.

When those first difficult words come at you—and they will—listen to them with a calmness that's rooted in your position in Christ. Don't immediately respond to criticism; instead, hear people out and be very, very quick to admit your own faults. Realize that God is using them for your sanctification, too.

Every criticism I've ever heard has offered something I needed to hear. It's in these difficult moments that your love for them can become the most visible and transformative.

3. Pray with them.

Pastoral ministry can be scary. There are many times that we care but we just don't know what to say. Thankfully, no matter the situation, we can always pray. Earnest prayer with your people is perhaps the most powerful tool for expressing your love while at the same time pointing them to the One who loves them perfectly.

4. Preach like you love them.

You'll exhibit your love for your people through careful, relationship-informed, gospel-soaked preaching. If you show them outside the pulpit that you care for them, then your expository ministry will flourish in the context of relationship. And that's powerful. When they hear and see you preach, do they see a man who's engaged in a labor of love? They should.

CONCLUSION

Looking at Jesus' words to Peter post-resurrection, we're reminded that the way we express our love for our Savior is through our love for his people. So, when laying the foundation for a new plant or revitalization, there's truly no better advice than this: "Before you do anything else, make sure your people know that you love them."

Like Peter, who had recently experienced the love of his Master, let the love of Christ control us to such a degree that we view the people in our charge differently. Let us love them as members of the body of the Savior we love, and that by loving him, we love them.

ABOUT THE AUTHOR
Steve Jennings is the pastor of Immanuel Church of Fujairah in the United Arab Emirates.

"The Loneliness of Church Planting"

John Starke

For the last decade or so, there's been a deepened interest in urban church planting. Young guys move into big cities with visions of planting "a church for the city." They want to live in the neighborhoods that many evangelical churches attempted to escape in previous decades.

In the 1990s, I remember first reading Jim Cymbala's *Fresh Wind, Fresh Fire*, about the renewal of The Brooklyn Tabernacle. I was mesmerized by the foreign world of 1980s New York City described in his stories. But Cymbala wasn't giving a vision *for the city*. He was relaying stories from the front lines.

Famous books about churches in New York City, like *Fresh Wind* or *The Cross and the Switchblade*, weren't calling for a renewed interest in moving to the city. They weren't encouraging intrepid young pastors to invest their lives there. Instead, they told exotic stories of a faraway land that, at best, excited youth group mission trips. And if you happened to get up and *move* to the city, you'd likely receive more warnings about the sexualized and liberal city than encouragements about the prospective good the Lord might do. "What about your kids?" you'd hear. "Do you want them growing up in that environment?"

A DIFFERENT TIME

But that was then. Things have changed. To be sure, my wife and I still received those warnings and side-eye glances, but that didn't characterize my experience. Now, newly minted ministers are coming to the city in droves. Now, it's common for churches in urban contexts to even have "City" in their name. Now, many churches distinguish themselves with their explicit city-oriented mission statements.

This renewed emphasis of urban church planting has even caused weariness among some evangelicals. The weariness isn't because they believe the city is evil, as previous generations may have, but because they've mistook the emphasis as a focus on the "elites" as opposed to the rural and suburban communities of fly-over states.

While I understand the concern, I'm less than sympathetic. In New York, we need *a thousand* churches planted over the next few decades. That's not an exaggeration. The renewed focus of church planting in cities, especially in NYC, is *only now beginning* to see some impact. We probably all know of great stories of churches coming and growing and seeing fruit in the city. But we need more than just a few success stories in a handful of churches. Right now, in Manhattan, only 2 to 4 percent of the population claims to be evangelical or "traditional" Christian. To get something close to 8 to 10 percent, we don't just need to hear of three or four great stories of growing churches in NYC; *we need 600*.

A CONCERN

Yet what may be of greater concern is what's actually drawing more pastors to the city. Some criticize the "for the city" vision so popular these days as working out to mean "for the white culturally elite of the city." I'm more sympathetic to that concern.

Even still, I think there's a more basic problem. Call it a pastoral hunch or a spiritual sense, but for many of us who pastor in places like NYC, we're enchanted by the city. After all, ministering to elites can mean being "associated with elites." Ministering to people who work on Broadway or at Google or Twitter or for fashion houses, *The New York Times*, and NPR can mean we'll be associated with people who work on Broadway or at Google or Twitter or for fashion houses, *The New York Times*, and NPR. None of us would ever explicitly say that, but we're often unaware of the desires of our hearts that drive us to do many of the things we do.

WHAT WE SHOULD TELL PROSPECTIVE CITY CHURCH PLANTERS

But what should be communicated to church planters is just how unattractive, humiliating, confusing, tiring, and lonely long-term church planting, revitalizing, and pastoring is, especially in the city. I probably talk to more homeless neighbors than "cultural elites." I spend more time calling and waiting for paramedics to help unconscious folks on our front steps than I do giving talks at the Googleplex.

Office space, if you can afford it, is often makeshift and uncomfortable. Big crowds and white-walled gallery events are primarily found on Instagram and Pinterest.

The transience is breathtaking, which makes "church growth" difficult on top of the already hostile environment. One close friend of mine just explained to me that he led 75 people through their membership class this year. This sounded like excellent news, since we'd been praying his church wouldn't have to close it doors because of finances. Yet due to the transient nature, his Sunday morning gathering attendance hasn't change a bit from last year.

This transience means church planters and revitalizers often struggle with a strange loneliness. Most friends you make will leave within a few years. I was having dinner with a pastor and his wife, and they explained that in the last 18 months they lost all of their closest friends. Pastors and their wives constantly have the experience of having to "start again" with relationships. That can be extremely weary.

Personally, I've struggled with depression for the first time in my life and have found a common experience among my colleagues. If you know the dynamics of depression, it exasperates the already difficult challenges of ministry.

Living spaces are expensive. A 1 to 2 bedroom apartment in Manhattan ranges from $3,300 to $4,000 per month. And yet most pastors I know serve churches that don't pay what they need to survive, take an occasional vacation, and save. Many pastors go into personal debt. The toll this can have on families is significant.

Before they move, many pastors and their wives aren't aware of how deep our expectations of comfort are, yet they quickly learn in their new, two-bedroom apartments that are 600–700 square feet with no backyard—not to mention the little-to-no family support. As a result, pastors are generally as transient as anyone in New York, and transient pastors aren't a great formula for church renewal.

An enchantment with the city isn't the same as a biblical love for the city, and it won't sustain you in the long run.

WHAT CITIES NEED

I don't write this in order to push away prospective pastors. Instead, I'm eager to see a generation of pastors who are aware of and have counted the cost, who have wives who know what it will take and what they will have to sacrifice.

Of course this is true not only in New York City.

My city and maybe yours needs pastors who know what failure feels like and how to respond to it so that they will persevere nevertheless. We need pastors with thick prayer lives and an awareness that they may be more insecure than they think.

Success in many churches means having a pastor who

knows how to experience rejection, criticism, and failure on Sunday, and yet get back up on Monday to pray and prepare yet another Sunday sermon. We need pastors who know how to feel forgettable and to trust God. We need pastors who know how to read their hearts and Bibles just as well as they know how to read the *New York Times*. We need pastors who learn from their mistakes and pray so that they might be better. We need pastors who will be hospitable and listen to their neighbors. We need pastors who pray for their people, pray for their neighbors, pray for the kingdom to come. Maybe then God will bless us and bring revival. The best pastors doing the best and most fruitful work are prayerful, humble, repentant, teachable, and very secure in Christ. We need so many more pastors like that.

ABOUT THE AUTHOR

John Starke is the lead pastor of Apostles Uptown in New York City. You can find him on Twitter at @john_starke.

The Blessings and Burdens of A Church Planter's Wife

Gloria Furman

No two church planting wives are the same. Our unique church contexts, seasons, personalities, challenges, gifts, perspectives, and preferences could fill volumes.

WHAT'S DIFFERENT

If you sat down for chai with Ananya in Ahmedabad and asked her to discuss the blessings and burdens of being a church planter's wife, she may have different things to say than Bonnie in Burnaby, Miriam in Niddrie, or Ana Clara in Sao Paulo. While I'm typing this in Dubai, certain blessings come right to mind—the extraordinary gift of worshiping Jesus with brothers and sisters from more than sixty nationalities and the overwhelming gratitude that members share even in difficult circumstances. Some burdens may include the daily pressure of navigating cultures in such a diverse context and the radiating desert sun that can zap your willpower and the battery in your car.

The loneliness and isolation that one church planting wife feels may seem like a welcome respite to a wife who compares herself to a goldfish swimming in a fishbowl surrounded by malicious cats. Concerning the spectrum of feelings about support-raising, one month may be like sharing an adventure and the next may introduce a suffocating strain on your marriage.

A wife's confidence in "the plan" to plant a church may waver—even by the hour (and years later). One woman's burden of acute stress in a new context or season may be a blessing in disguise as she learns to depend on the Lord for strength. For others, acute stress may be a red flag to change course.

The unofficial welcome committee may or may not roll out the red carpet for the minister's family. I once heard a story about someone who called the school registrar and impersonated the pastor's wife and took her kids' names off the waitlist for next term. Another church planting wife says she has a closet full of the gifts that people keep bringing them.

One church planting wife may already be packing the house when her church planting husband looks to the horizon and wants to keep planting, and another may feel disappointed.

Persecution may be woven in with spiritual victory over demonic forces; anxiety may stand out on the backdrop of comfort and ease. These and many more contexts, seasons, personalities, challenges, perspectives, and preferences contribute to our uniqueness as church planting wives.

WHAT'S THE SAME

But some things are the same no matter who you are, what time period you live in, and where God has called your family to plant a church. For one, the conclusion is the same. By faith we all see how our various blessings and burdens are braided together in God's hand as he only gives us everything needful for our good and his glory.

As she surveys the landscape of her blessings and burdens, the conclusion of every church planting wife is this: *Blessed be the God and Father of our Lord Jesus Christ who has blessed us with every spiritual blessing in the heavenly places in Christ Jesus.* All of the unique factors mentioned above—every single one of them—can and do change. But God and his Word do not change, and the light of this truth illuminates our perspective on all those changeable things.

Church planting wives need to have the light of God's Word shine on their various blessings and burdens. We need this like we need the sun to rise. We need the light in order to go about doing what we need to do. Two things happen when you turn on the lights in the kitchen. One, you can clearly see what you're doing (and where the coffee pot is). And two, if there happen to be any cockroaches having a slumber party, they'll scatter. When God's Word turns the lights on for us, so-to-speak, we see reality and the contaminating lies disappear. Blessings and burdens need to be held up to the light of the Word.

APPLICATION

Here are a few floodlights of unchanging truth that every church planting wife can apply:

1. Jesus, the Chief Shepherd, has been given all authority in heaven and on earth and gives his disciples his mission with his blessing and presence (Matt. 28:18–20). Issues surrounding calling, priority, and fear are all resolved when church planting wives look to Christ and recall Jesus' utterly comprehensive *authority* to tell us what we're to be about doing, his contagious *zeal* to spread the glory of God among all nations, and his unassailable *power* to provide for us and never leave us as we go about that work.

2. By the grace of Jesus alone can a church planting wife walk in love together with the under-shepherd whom she married (Eph. 5). As they walk with Christ together, they'll find themselves outside the camp where Christ is, and only with the help of Jesus will they bear the reproach Christ endured. However much they love (or don't love) their city, the husband and wife know their home isn't dependent on his job because they're seeking the city that is to come. When push comes to shove, as they say, and like Paul the church planting husband undergoes "the daily pressure on me of my anxiety for all the churches," the church planting wife takes her cue to boast with her husband of the things that show their weakness and Christ's strength.

3. Jesus loves his Bride, the church, and not even the gates of hell will prevail against her (Matt. 16:18, Eph. 5:25–27). Identity, gifting, and commitment issues are resolved when church planting wives look to Christ and see how he has made them to be a brick in the building, a sheep in the flock, a priest in the priesthood, and a member of the family. All of these metaphors light up the sparks in her Scripture-soaked imagination as she dreams up ways to build up the body of Christ with the gifts given to her by the ascended Lord Jesus.

Blessings and burdens mingle together as we live in this world that groans for the Day of redemption—now several minutes closer than it was at the start of this article. There's no way a finite heart can hold all the things a church planting wife will face in life and ministry. But Christ can, he does, and he will.

ABOUT THE AUTHOR

Gloria Furman is the author of *Alive in Him: How Being Embraced by the Love of Christ Changes Everything, Missional Motherhood*. She lives in Dubai with her four children and husband, Dave.

Stop Launching Churches! Instead, Covenant Together

Nathan Knight

I think we should stop talking about "launching" new church plants and instead refer to them "covenanting" for the first time.

WHY DO WE SAY "LAUNCH"?

I am a church planter myself. I've learned from other planters, talked to planters, read updates from planters, and read the books on church planting. And we all say "launch."

Why?

I asked a few. Their responses were not all the same. The most common definition I have heard is, "This is the date on which our planting team 'goes public.'" When I follow up by asking if a person from the public could have attended their meetings before the "launch" the common answer is "sure."

So what actually happened when you "launched," if people from the public could have attended before? Apparently, launching is different than having a child or getting married. You *know* when those things happen!

Here's what I think we planters have done: borrowed a word from the business world in order to garner energy and inject life into a church from its beginning.

HOW ABOUT "COVENANT" INSTEAD?

I would like to advocate the use of the biblical word "covenant" to designate the beginning of a church, as in "We first covenanted as a congregation on June 24."

You find a picture of the returning exiles renewing their covenant with each other and God in Nehemiah 9:32-38. And the fellowship of a church is a kind of covenant, whereby we affirm one another's professions of faith and agree to oversee one another's discipleship to Christ. This is the cumulative picture that you see in Matthew 16 when Jesus affirms Peter and Peter's profession (v. 17), and that you see again (in inverse form) in Matthew 18 when the church removes its affirmation of someone's profession of faith (v. 17).

What is a church? It's a gathering of two or three people in Christ's name—a society of people covenanted together in the same gospel profession. Through baptism and the Lord's Supper we partake of this local covenant together as our localized picture of our new covenant membership. (Bobby Jamieson, in his brand new book *Going Public*, describes baptism as the *initiating oath sign of the new covenant*. And he describes the Lord's Supper as the *renewing oath sign of the new covenant*.)

I don't think Scripture compels us to use the word "covenanting" to speak about the beginning of a church. It doesn't tell us we must. I'm not saying that either. I do think the word helpfully captures what happens in Scripture when a group of Christians organize as a church. Therefore I'm offering it as a "best practice."

NOT JUST TRADING ONE WORD FOR ANOTHER

"Covenanting" is more than just trading one word for another word. It communicates the idea that certain actions must take place in order to establish a church, just like a wedding ceremony demands certain actions take place in order for a man and a woman to come together under the covenant of marriage.

First, covenanting demands that *a particular set of expectations* bind a group of Christians together, like biblical vows place a set of expectations on husband and wife. They are responsible to affirm one another's gospel professions. And they are responsible to oversee one another's discipleship.

Secondly, covenanting demands that a particular set of expectations bind *a particular group of Christians*. It makes clear who is meaningfully part of the church and who is not. We are a people "set apart" from the world.

How thin and meaningless the word "launch" seems by comparison! Covenant is a family word, a blood oath word. Launch is a rocketship word, or a widget factory word.

Finally, the word covenant communicates the idea that the church is a people, not an "event."

THE OLD MEETINGHOUSES

If you were to walk into the back of the old meetinghouses (as they called them) where churches gathered, you would sometimes find a beautiful document called a church covenant. It would lay out a way of life that the church had agreed to live by. At the bottom would be the signatures of the church's members.

I don't want to make too big a deal about what we call the beginning of a church. But I do think the word covenant will help to shepherd our people into a richer, deeper, and more biblical picture of what the life of the local church is and what it's not. Which suggests it just may be a practice worth recapturing.

ABOUT THE AUTHOR

Nathan Knight is the pastor of Restoration Church in Washington, D. C.

The Calculated Risks of Church Planting: Sending Your Best Members and Elders

Juan Sanchez

"If you had to do it all over again, would you still do it?"

That sounds like a question you might ask someone who's just been convicted of a crime, and it's one I was asked just this morning. My crime? Sending off 37 of our best members, along with two of our best elders, to plant a church. The prosecutor? An elder of a brand new church plant in Dubai. I had just shared with him how much our latest church plant cost us.

We can always find reasons, even good ones, for not planting a church. And yet, the need for church planting in my town (Austin, Texas) far outweighs whatever adverse effects we may face.

OUR NEED TO PLANT ANOTHER CHURCH

We didn't need to plant another church because we were bursting at the seams. We still have plenty of room in our building. We didn't plant another church because we possess abundant financial resources. We have an overwhelming debt that hangs like a millstone around our necks. Instead, we needed to plant a church for pastoral and evangelistic reasons.

First, we had a significant number of members who were driving from northwest Austin to gather with us each week. That's at least a 30-minute drive for most of them. When members live that far away, it's hard to "shepherd the flock of God among you" (1 Pet. 5:2). We struggled to foster gospel community among our membership because distance became a logistical obstacle. Second, those members who lived far away found it hard to build gospel relationships with neighbors and invite them to our gatherings.

But not only did we need to plant a church, our city needed us to plant another church. Between 2005 and 2015, metro Austin grew by almost 38%, surpassing 2 million people. In fact, from July 1, 2015 to July 1, 2016, the metro Austin population increased by 58,301. That's about 164 people per day. Such growth means church planting efforts in our city aren't keeping up with population growth. In our context, we cannot afford NOT to plant a church.

OUR CALCULATED RISK IN PLANTING ANOTHER CHURCH

So then, understanding our pastoral and evangelistic concerns, and our city's need, we took a calculated risk and planted another church. There's never a good time to plant a church. You'll always find valid, even logical reasons for putting it off. In our case, though, we realized that many of our reasons for not planting were grounded in fear. We were afraid of losing members, finances, and leaders.

Much to our surprise, we felt the effects of planting a church almost immediately. Previously, we had eight elders for just over 500 members. The December before we planted, one of our elders rotated off the elder board.

In February of the following year, our new church plant held their first public meetings. In a period of just over two months we went from eight elders to five. And once the church plant officially received new members, we removed those we had sent from our membership: a total of 37.

Don't get me wrong. We weren't just interested in the numbers. But those numbers represented some of our best members and strongest givers. Consequently, over the next year we began to feel the void. Our five remaining elders found it hard to care for our almost 500 members. Though we were wise to reduce our new budget by 10% to account for the calculated loss in income, our giving wasn't as strong as we'd hoped. At this point, planting that new church seemed like a foolish decision.

So, if we had to do it again, would we still do it? Absolutely!

THE BLESSINGS OF PLANTING A CHURCH

As always, God is faithful. When we sent off 37 of our best members in February 2015, we asked God to send us 37 new members over the next year. The Lord answered our prayers. He caused the growth (1 Cor. 3:6), and by the end of 2015, we had received 74 new members. As we observed God's kindness, we were encouraged in our decision to plant a church. Had we not planted a new church, we would have missed out on the joy of answered prayer for new members.

Unfortunately, the addition of new members didn't offset our financial deficit. We thought reducing our budget by 10%, along with new member growth, would address our financial needs. We were wrong.

But, again, God is faithful! Several months into the life of the new church plant, they had more money than we did. Understanding our financial situation, they asked us to stop providing them financial support. Though we rejoiced in their financial freedom and were thankful for their generosity, that financial relief was not enough to keep our church from financial hardship. By the fall of our new church plant's second year, we found ourselves in a significant financial deficit.

We were approximately $130,000.00 behind our budget. After much deliberation, our elders agreed to go before the congregation and let them know of our need. In addition to our normal weekly need of about $28,000.00, the elders proposed a one day special offering with a $100,000.00 goal. By God's grace, our members responded in overflowing generosity. We received just over $105,000.00 for the special offering, and about $48,000.00 for our regular weekly offering. Had we not planted a new church, we would never have known God's grace through the generosity of our members (2 Cor. 8:1–5).

Finally, we still had a need for more leaders (2 Tim. 2:2). Because of the burden of so few elders caring for so many members, we asked God for more elders. As always, we continued identifying elder-qualified men in the congregation. But now, we sensed a greater urgency. Having prayed regularly and tested men diligently, we identified several younger men in our congregation who were qualified. One year after planting the church, the elder that had previously rotated off returned, bringing us to six elders. We also identified another five men we believed were qualified. Though for various reasons two of those men were unable to serve at that time, three of them were. Over that next year, the church affirmed all three of them, and, as of today, we have nine elders. Had we not planted a church, we may not have moved on these men with urgency, but each of these brothers has proven to be a valuable addition to our eldership.

CONCLUSION

There's no question in my mind that we would do it all over again. This is now our third church plant. By the end of 2017, we hope to plant a fourth– an Ethiopian congregation that will reach out to the Amharic-speaking population in metro Austin.

To be sure, not every context is the same; not every town is growing like Austin; not every church will be blessed in the same ways. But, after planting these churches, the Lord has taught us that not only does our city need us to keep planting churches, but, for the health of our church, we need to keep planting churches. And that would be true whether or not we continue to grow, increase our budget, and raise an abundance of new leaders. No matter the costs and effects of church planting on the planting church, the Lord is always faithful.

ABOUT THE AUTHOR

Juan Sanchez is the preaching pastor of High Pointe Baptist Church in Austin, Texas. You can find him on Twitter at @manorjuan.

What 9Marks Purists Should Know About Planting?

Ed Stetzer

When Jonathan Leeman asked me to write an article for this issue, he sent the title above and saying, "C'mon, don't you love the title?"

You see, he knows (and Mark Dever knows as well) that I love gospel clarity and biblical ecclesiology, but I'm concerned about the anti-practical nature we sometimes see in the 9Marks community.

This article is not in my place, but rather in yours, at their request, because they know I share so much in common. As a matter of fact, the last few churches I planted all used *A Display of God's Glory* to describe our polity. But I do think that there are some issues to consider in church planting. So, I've created nine things that 9Marks purists should know, because nine is a holy number!

1. PREACHING DOES NOT PLANT CHURCHES.

Your preaching is not as important as you think it is, at least in church planting.

Now, don't be a hater yet—keep in mind that this is a conversation about church planting. Let me be clear, preaching the Scriptures exegetically and theologically accurate is essential, meaningful, and vital to the health of your church, but it is not the first thing you do. You must also build relationships, share the gospel, and start groups.

You evangelize a church into existence, and then you start preaching to the church of the newly evangelized.

Yes, preaching and teaching are marks of a biblical church, but it is not how you plant a church. Preaching is a part of how you pastor a church— but you have to plant it (through evangelism) first.

Now, if you start with a group being sent out, and it's already a functioning church, that's another story on preaching—but it's the same story on evangelism. Evangelism has to be a driver if it is really church planting and not just hiving off a new preaching point.

Too many purists love preaching more than planting (and sometimes more than people), leading to a "plant" that is usually more about people wanting better and more Reformed preaching.

2. PRACTICAL MINISTRY AND PRAGMATISM ARE NOT THE SAME THING.

Never plant a church in your head.

For theorists and theologians, there is a danger of adopting methodology and modes of church planting without an understanding of your specific culture or context. We need a vision for the people God is calling us to, which means we must know them and then develop practical steps to actually plant a church among them. These practical steps can be as simple as meeting every neighbor on your street, inviting people to come with you to church, attending community events, etc. Church planting can't stay in the clouds, it has to make the practical jump to the streets.

And, what you heard in a conference or in seminary is not always the same as it is practically applied and lived out when you are planting from the inner city to the rural farmland.

3. YOU PLANT BY ENGAGING THE LOST, NOT BY IMMERSING IN CHURCH CULTURE.

You cannot live and love like Jesus without spending significant time with the people who don't know him.

Jesus said he came to "seek and save the lost" (Luke 19:10), and we are called to join Him on His mission. As a church planter, it's surprising that making and protecting time to spend with people who need to hear about Jesus is difficult, but it is. It can be easy to drift into the mode of teaching others fantastic methodology on seeking out those who are lost, but spend little time modeling it ourselves. This can create a church of intellectually well-equipped yet completely inexperienced missionaries. As church planters, with the various demands on your time, you must viciously protect the time you spend with friends, neighbors, and co-workers (if you're bivocational) who don't yet know Jesus. Modeling this, and doing it together with members of your church plant, will mold your culture around mission.

For a lot of purists, they have immersed themselves in a church or religious culture. Have you ever noticed how easy it is for us to start saying spiritually sounding phrases around people who are not spiritually inclined? That's a sign of church culture, not biblical truth, and certainly not knowing and engaging with normal people.

4. CULTURAL ENGAGEMENT IS BOTH CRUCIAL AND NOT NATURAL FOR THE THEOLOGICALLY INCLINED

You want to be both theologically astute and culturally engaged in order to plant a church effectively.

Sometimes, the people who are more adept at cultural engagement tend to be less theologically inclined, but that is not always a correlation. Often those who have studied theology for years find themselves missing cultural context clues, and their preaching is distant and disparate.

Planting a church well involves exegeting the culture God has sovereignly placed you in. This takes time, energy, effort, and intentionality. We must preach Christ and the Scriptures with a faithful understanding of theology, but we must also communicate in the language and cultural context of our time. I find it ironic that those who love the Puritans sometimes betray the Puritan practice of "speaking plainly."

You can be and should be both engaged in culture and theologically driven in your approach to ministry.

5. YOU WON'T PREACH AND DISCIPLE YOUR WAY TO EVANGELISM. YOU MUST LEAD YOUR CHURCH TO EVANGELISM BY ENGAGING IN EVANGELISM WITH THEM.

It is a myth that preaching and teaching will always produce an evangelistic church. It often doesn't.

Good teaching in isolation rarely has a transformative effect, though people tell me all that time that's their plan. A preacher's sermons must be matched by the activities of his life (1 Tim. 4:16; 2 Tim. 3:10). Watching you actively attend to your own and their evangelism, pastor, is the illustration your sermon's need to create a new culture. Evangelism needs to be caught and taught.

I actually had a discussion with one 9 Marks purist (did I mention that was Jonathan's phrase?) about that very thing. He was frustrated that he was teaching and preaching, discipling and going deeper, but evangelism was not increasing.

He agreed to do whatever I suggested for a few months. So, we planned outreach days, started a new series that was easy for Christians to bring guests (and then planned a bring-a-friend emphasis), planned church-wide outreach into the community, organized a prayer strategy, and more.

The end result? He did nothing that violated his purist views (that was our deal), yet soon the church was growing because it was mobilized and God was blessing.

6. YOU CAN LEARN FROM PEOPLE WHO ARE REACHING PEOPLE.

I often tell people that if they want to get a bad reputation for their church, start growing. Pastors who lead churches that aren't growing will find ways to explain away other churches' growth as illegitimate.

Yes, there are false converts. Yes, there are bad methodologies. No, we don't want to be momentum dependent. But, maybe you can learn more by asking, "What can I learn from someone who is reaching people that I am not reaching?"

7. LOVE JESUS.
8. PREACH THE GOSPEL.
9. CARE ABOUT ECCLESIOLOGY.

OK, I assumed we all would agree on the last three. And I wanted you to know that I'm with you on so much.

When Mark and I discussed this one day, I told him (in, I hope, a nice way) I believed he was creating a whole generation of theologically-minded but practically uninformed pastors that are less effective than they could be.

He responded something like, they are reading all the practical books (and, he graciously said many of them were mine). However, I am not convinced that is always the case. (And, Mark, your books sell a whole lot more than mine.)

But, in his answer, I found my hope. Mark is assuming you are getting the practical from somewhere. My concern is that 9 Marks purists are not—and need to.

So, learn best practices, learn how to engage the lost, learn how to lead your church well to engage its community, but don't do so by moving away from the gospel, the scriptures, and a biblical understanding of church.

That's my exhortation to you... my friends, 9Marks purists!

EDITOR'S NOTE
At 9Marks, we've long appreciated those with whom we have the most important things in common, yet disagree with us constructively (Prov. 27:6). This article by Ed Stetzer is an example of putting that appreciation into practice. We hope you'll benefit from him, just as we have.

ABOUT THE AUTHOR
Ed Stetzer holds the Billy Graham Chair of Church, Mission, and Evangelism at Wheaton College and serves as Executive Director of the Billy Graham Center for Evangelism.

Church Planting in the Same Building

Matthew
Spandler-Davison

On Sunday morning, as I sit in my office to prepare for worship, I can hear the muffled sounds of singing and preaching coming from the main hall in our building. Pre-school aged children are playing in the classroom next to my office. The aroma of brewed coffee comes from the kitchen. Communion cups have already been prepared.

And yet . . . no one from our church has arrived. Instead, at 8:30am on a Sunday morning, members of Grace Fellowship Church in Bardstown, Kentucky, have gathered for their weekly worship gathering. It's a church we planted, and it's a church with whom we're delighted to share our property.

We planted a church in our own building.

THE STORY

In 2012, the elders of Bardstown Christian Fellowship (my church) presented to our members a proposal for what we termed "On-Site Church Planting." The early years of Bardstown Christian Fellowship, a church planted south of Louisville, were difficult. Evangelism proved an uphill struggle in an area where only one in 10 people are active in church, and half are Roman Catholic. The church experienced slow but steady growth over the first decade. In 2011, the elders recognized we'd soon outgrow our meeting space. We had little enthusiasm for spending more money on a bigger building. Neither did we have any desire to start a second worship service. So, committed to reaching the lost through church planting, the elders were led to start a second church.

What we did next is unusual. We planted this second church in the same building. Two churches, one location. One meets at 8:30, the other at 11:00

We launched Grace Fellowship Church in August 2012. We commissioned three of our elders and a number of families to start this new work. We started the BCF Network, which owns the property and its furnishings. The member churches have equal access to the property. As churches, we've pooled our resources so that we hold everything in common. We jointly fund a church administrator, and we share the expenses of the facilities. This is our long-term strategy, to make the facility available as a public space in which like-minded churches can gather for worship and partner together to reach our city and the nations.

Grace Fellowship (the newer church) has already celebrated a number of baptisms and is connecting with people we never reached. We're convinced our community in central Kentucky doesn't need more church buildings, but more healthy churches. Churches in small-town America already own enough properties; they just need to be more strategic in how we're using them.

THE RATIONALE: WHAT IS A CHURCH

Many pastors I've shared this story with have raised their hands up in complete confusion. They ask, "Why would you do that? "In order to best understand the rationale for the creation of a property-sharing network of churches, it's first necessary to be clear about what a church is. Most Christians would acknowledge a church is not a building but the people—and yet, when we strip away a building from a church, we begin to question the legitimacy or viability of that church.

A growing church has options to consider when dealing with practical issues related to space and organization. Many would consider starting multiples services or campuses. However, to do so distorts the very nature of the church.

Jesus uses the word *ekklesia* when referring to the church in Matthew 18:17. When a brother sins against another brother and does not repent, then a decision is deferred to the gathered congregation of believers, the *ekklesia*, to remove him from that local and visible body of believers. In using the term, Jesus indicates that the act of assembling together as one group is integral to the authority and identity of a particular church. In Matthew 18, Christ grants authority to the identifiable assembly of Christians to determine who is, or is not, a member of the church. Multiple assemblies, therefore, suggest multiple churches.

Jonathan Leeman puts it this way,

"What shall we say constitutes a local church on earth? The answer which the Bible gives, I think, is simple and straightforward: a local church is constituted by a group of Christians gathering together bearing Christ's own authority in the gospel to exercise the power of the keys of binding and loosing through the ordinances."

A church then, as Leeman correctly points out, is a gathering of Christians that exercises the authority given to it in order to fulfill the mission it has received so that it be a display of Christ to the watching world. A group that doesn't regularly gather at one time and in one place is therefore not a church as understood by the use of the term *ekklesia* in Matthew 18.

This understanding of the church as being a visible assembly of believers that worship together is key to understanding the rationale for Bardstown Christian Fellowship and our choice to develop a network of churches rather than starting multiple services or sites.

YOU COULD DO IT, TOO

Many growing churches are in towns and cities where members drive by many other church buildings in order to get to their own church service. In other words, just because a church meets in a particular neighborhood doesn't mean it will only effectively reach that particular neighborhood. Furthermore, sending a group of believers to a separate location necessitates duplicating resources and investing funds in new accommodations and equipment, funds that could perhaps be better spent on missions and ministry.

Acknowledging this, a growing church might consider a new gathering place or building a larger building. This is a perfectly reasonable response to growth—though it's often a costly one. A church gathering in a city with extremely high property values, or a church meeting in a nation where it's difficult to own property, will find this option increasingly out of reach.

I simply want to offer an alternative to a costly building campaign or tying up resources in more bricks and mortar. That alternative is establishing of a network of churches that partner together to share property and resources, and support each other in the work of the ministry.

The Bardstown Christian Fellowship of Churches is an example of just that: a network of likeminded churches that share the same property, jointly fund administrative staff, and work together to make disciples of all nations.

ABOUT THE AUTHOR
Matthew Spandler-Davison is the pastor of Redeemer Fellowship Church in Bardstown, Kentucky, and the director of the BCF Network and Urban Impact Missions.

Lessons Learned from Church-Planting by Peaceable Division

Colin Clark

In September we did something crazy: we planted a church on the other side of our city.

Or maybe that doesn't sound crazy. But hold on. We planted by literally *dividing our church in half*, and we did this as a relatively small and young church.

We didn't grow to 800 and send out 30. Our three-year old church had 84 members before the plant, and 45 after. Our financial giving was reduced by more than fifty percent. Pre-plant, there were four families in my apartment complex; post-plant, only my family remained.

That very same week, there was an article here at 9Marks called "Church Planting by Peaceable Division." To call it timely would be a massive understatement. The article highlights the historical prevalence of churches intentionally and amicably splitting for the proclamation of the gospel and the glory of God.

This is what we did, and I offer six lessons we learned from the process.

(1) God leads even young, small churches to plant; it's not a mission merely for large, established churches.

Even as we were walking through our decision, there was something in me that fought back against it. Why? Well, we hadn't had time to "come into our own" yet. We could always use more elders and more leaders, not to mention people in general! Our budget could be healthier. We could always teach on church planting a bit more.

All of those hesitancies should be weighed seriously. If you are going to ask your congregation to do something painful, they need to understand the *why*. It's good stewardship to consider budgets, and it's wise to consider leadership capacity. But logistics can become too important, and hinder churches from obedience.

At our church, we were quickly approaching size constraints. We looked at a map of our city and realized nearly half of our folks were travelling to the northeast part of the city, where we meet, from the southwest. Some even drove three hours round-trip. So we push ahead. Maybe God is calling your church to plant before you're ready, too?

But why not just secure a bigger facility or start a satellite campus in the southeast? That leads to a second lesson.

(2) The heat of planting tests and reveals a church's ecclesiological priorities.

"To plant or not to plant" will always drive us to ask why we exist as a church. Is our ultimate goal comfortable community or missional community? How important is it that our church members live in proximity to their church and other church members? Do we more highly value having our act together in one place before reaching out to another? How highly do we value financial sustainability at the "mother church" before sending healthy members out from us? Do we desire to grow one big church in one neighborhood or to have two smaller churches in two neighborhoods? Do we think the local church is an assembly, or do we want think it is viable to have multiple locations and call them one church? What about "protecting our DNA"—popular nomenclature these days—and our preaching ministry? Do we care about that? And if so, how much?

I'm not trying to tell you how each of those questions should be answered. I'm just saying this is a huge lesson in church planting—and you should be ready for it. Your priorities will be put on an operating table for everyone to poke and examine. You'll have to answer questions you didn't even know were questions and to question things you thought you'd already answered!

(3) Church planting *reinforces gospel motivation.*

This one wasn't really on my radar, honestly, but it was a pleasant surprise. Our plant reinforced gospel motivation—and not just in the obvious ways about how we want more people to hear God's Word and be exposed to gospel witness.

What I mean is, it made *me* realize that the gospel must be the driving force behind each young man I disciple, each person I evangelize, each couple I counsel our living room couch. Once you decide to be a church-planting church—and especially if you plant by peaceable division—it's far too easy to be far too "strategic" with your time. We all have boundaries and filters, to be sure, but should I keep counseling this couple when I know they'll be heading to the church plant in three months? Should I keep building into this potential elder when he'll likely be an elder in the other church and not mine?

Of course I should! And I should because the point of ministry isn't building my own kingdom; it's building God's. I'd hope the gospel would motivate me regardless, but the process of planting reinforced it for me.

(4) Church planting by peaceable division *presents unique pastoral challenges.*

Let me list a few:

- Your elders have to lead courageously like never before. Emotionally, nobody wants to plant and it will almost certainly stall out unless you have leaders out front with the standard.
- Your elders need to be on the same page about how to counsel members. There will be a ton of questions: *Should I stay or go? What if one church is closer to my home but the other is closer to my work? When do I have to make a decision? What is the process if I want to go? What things should I consider if I'm equidistant to both churches? What if I'm closer to one church but my mom's group will end up at the other church? Do I just get to pick or are the elders making a recommendation about where I should go?* The questions will come. Be ready.
- If you're planting by peaceable division, both churches will feel like church plants for a while. Help members think about the needs at both churches as they're making their decisions.
- Get on the same page with other elders and communicate well. Will any elders be "recruiting" for either church? Do we want this to happen at one church but not the other? Who are some of the key leaders each pastor is hoping to have on their team once the dust settles? Over-communicate on the front end and talk through as much as you can—it will serve you well.
- One of the biggest challenges for me was that I processed the reality of the plant far earlier than everyone else. This caused me to be less empathetic once the plant happened. I had mentally moved on while many of our members were dealing with it afresh. As a result, I'm not sure I was in a good place to shepherd them as well as I could have.

These are just a few of the unique challenges and opportunities. You'll have your own; be reflective and patient.

(5) Church planting *is an opportunity for Satan*.

This one is obvious, but church planting accompanies unique temptation for division, disputes, and hurt feelings. Be on the lookout for opportunities Satan may use to drive relational wedges that cause disunity. We should always give the benefit of the doubt to our friends, assume godly motives among godly leaders, and be wary of the sin in our own hearts.

Any time there's a plant, Satan will tempt Church A to keep a watchful eye on Church B. This is good insofar as the "mother church" want to make sure the plant is growing in the joy of the Lord and remains free from false gospels. Yet churches must guarded against competitiveness, or being suspicious anytime the other church does something new or different.

While we're certainly not perfect, we've worked to remain on the "same team." Both churches frequently pray for each other publicly during the morning and evening gatherings. We share pulpits with each other. If we bring a guest speaker in town, we try to share. We invite each other to events, conferences, and some retreats. We formed an association (our two churches plus others) to band together for pastoral training, church planting, and missions. Be on the lookout for ways Satan will use this for *his* good, and fight the good fight.

(6) Church planting *is really hard but really worth it*.

I'll put it all together in one final lesson: church planting by peaceable division was really, really hard, but also really, really worth it. The biggest struggles for us involved emotional difficulties: friendships complicated, healthy community shaken up. The smaller your church and the deeper your community, the bigger this struggle will be.

And to that, we say, "Praise God!" What a great problem to have! This is true, but it also doesn't make the struggle any less real or difficult.

On top of that came the difficulties of not having enough elders, deacons, and money. Our church was left with less experienced preachers; we also lost a majority of the large families. I could go on because the list of challenges isn't short.

But for all the burdens, we experienced far more blessings. On any given Sunday, our churches have attenders from six of the seven continents, and they'll all hear the gospel. Our church in the northeast has had more room for more people to come in and hear God's Word proclaimed, and the plant in the southwest has been able to provide a healthy church for many who hadn't heard of our church or who had but didn't want to make the hour-plus trek across the city. We've also been able to start an association that seeks to strengthen even more local churches.

On a personal level, the whole experience of church planting strengthened my faith. I had to trust God like never before and take my hands off situations that, in my flesh, I so greatly wanted to manipulate. God met me—and all of us—in the midst of any confusion, and truly gave us peace that surpasses understanding.

May it be so for you as well. Pray for us—that we'd be willing, joyful, and expectant should God entrust us with such an opportunity again.

ABOUT THE AUTHOR

Colin Clark is the senior pastor of an international church in China. You can find him on Twitter at @jasoncseville.

How to Do Ministry When You Don't Have Money

Brian Davis

How do you do ministry when you don't have any money? How do you serve the Lord as a church planter while broke? After 30 years of experience, I assure you I have expertise. But wisdom comes from Scripture:

Keep your life free from love of money, and be content with what you have, for he has said, "I will never leave you nor forsake you." So we can confidently say,

> "The Lord is my helper; I will not fear; what can man do to me?" (Heb. 13:5–6)

The text teaches us four things about doing ministry without money.

1. Be Careful
2. Be Content
3. Be Creative
4. Be Confident

1. BE CAREFUL ("KEEP YOUR LIFE FREE FROM LOVE OF MONEY…")

Pastors and church planters should watch their souls closely. Our ministries should be without covetousness, which Colossians 3 calls idolatry. The Bible pushes pastors in particular here, as an elder must not be a "lover of money" (1 Tim. 3:3).

Money is useful and has its benefits. It's good for churches to pay their pastor so as not to muzzle the ox (1 Tim. 5:18). But don't long for money or trust in it, or equate the size of your budget with the power of God. Money measures neither God's ability nor the value of our efforts. Jesus warns us plainly, "No one can serve two masters…You cannot serve God and money."

Also, just because you don't have money doesn't mean you don't love it. If you grumble in your lack, your heart posture may not be service for Jesus but an inordinate affection for money.

A good litmus test for church planters is this: is your willingness to serve dependent on the pay? Remember Paul's parting words to the Ephesian elders:

> "I coveted no one's silver or gold or apparel. You yourselves know that these hands ministered to my necessities and to those who were with me. In all things I have shown you that by working hard in this way we must help the weak and remember the words of the Lord Jesus, how he himself said, 'It is more blessed to give than to receive'" (Acts 20:33–35).

2. BE CONTENT ("…AND BE CONTENT WITH WHAT YOU HAVE…")

Living without covetousness means being content with what you have. "Be satisfied with the present," says another translation. We rest in the providence and provision of God, knowing this: "I will never leave you nor forsake you." Pastor, how do you deal with not having money? You should think on the fact that you have God!

Worry only has one remedy: a mindfulness of God. God encourages us to ask for what we don't have, but then we're free to trust whatever he gives or doesn't (Matt. 6; Phil 4:5–7).

So, does your ministry need more funding? Are there currently unmet needs? Paul's own support letter gives us the secret to contentment:

> I have learned in whatever situation I am to be content. I know how to be brought low, and I know how to abound. In any and every circumstance, I have learned the secret of facing plenty and hunger, abundance and need. I can do all things *through him who strengthens me*" (Phil 4:11-13).

If we're known and loved by Jesus, our situation can never improve because our status will never change. He has pledged himself to us. And his Great Commission hangs not on our bank accounts but on the fact that he possesses all authority on heaven and on earth, and he is with us.

C. S. Lewis put it this way: "He who has God and everything else has no more than he who has God only."

Hebrews tells us that Jesus is the Son of God, the appointed heir of all things. He is preeminent. He is rich in possessions and power. All things were made for him, and through him the world was created—things on heaven and things on earth. The universe is upheld by the word of his power! He's seated at the right hand of majesty on High—not a chair, but a throne: "Your throne, O God, is forever and ever."

It's this same ruling and reigning Lord who is with us even now.

God sometimes denies our requests now to prepare us for permanent joy in glory. If God gave us everything we wanted, then we'd trust our things more than him. Do you not pray most when you need most?

Pastors and planters, be mature in your thinking: "He who did not spare his own Son but gave him up for us all, how will he not also with him graciously give us all things?" If he hasn't given you something, his denial is a gift. He owns all, he knows what's best, and he loves you.

3. BE CREATIVE

Spurgeon in his book, *Lectures to My Students* has a section where he marvels at the abilities of some to accomplish exceptional good with very humble means. Spurgeon humorously labels ministers who are broke as workers with "slender apparatus." He writes, "Work away, then, poor brother, for you may succeed in doing great things in your ministry, and if so, your welcome of 'Well done, good and faithful servant,' will be all the more emphatic because you labored under serious difficulties."

So, rather than bemoaning what you can't do, enjoy what you can do.

To restate the question from the beginning: How do you do stuff when you don't have money? Brothers, you simply do what you can do.

And guess what? The most powerful and important things you can do are all *free*! Prayer is free! Studying Scripture is free! Sharing the gospel is free! Gathering for fellowship is free! Admonishing the idle, encouraging the weary and faint-hearted, and helping the weak is free!

Sometimes, the blessing of God in denying us resources is him removing the very things our hearts are tempted to trust in. And is it not true that in our lack we often learn how much we still have?

Be as creative as the book of God permits you, and then go and battle in his name! Like King David, we don't go armed from the armory of the world—no, our stones from the brook are promises from the Word of God.

4. BE CONFIDENT.

The Lord is our helper, and as Philippians tells us, "God will supply every need according to his riches in glory in Christ Jesus."

Who is it that is with us? Hebrews offers a massive view of God, and if we're to be comforted and confident it will require that our theology is equally robust.

Finally, we must never forget it is our Lord's wisdom that assigns one talent to some, two talents to some, and five talents to others. We should also note that our Lord is not unreasonable. Charles Spurgeon is not more sympathetic to our situation than the Sovereign Lord who assigned it to us. If he has limited your resources, then he will not enlarge his expectations. No, he is looking for those of us to whom he has given little, to be faithful over little.

ABOUT THE AUTHOR

Brian Davis lives in Philadelphia with his wife, Sonia, and their two sons, Spurgeon and Sibbes. He is part of the church planting team for Risen Christ Fellowship. You can find him on Twitter at @theservantfella.

Church Planting across Ethnic Lines

Joel Kurz

Nine years ago, my wife and I (both of us white) moved into a neighborhood where we were an ethnic minority. We wanted to plant a church. Over the years, our idealism has been crushed, we've hit rock bottom, experienced a rebirth of vision, and have slowly made progress. God has been incredibly kind as he has formed a diverse church in our neighborhood. The immediate context is mostly African-American, yet we're three blocks from a historically white neighborhood. Our church is about half black, half white, and maybe two percent Asian.

BIBLICAL BASIS

First and foremost: it's biblical and right to do cross-cultural ministry. God does burden individuals from one culture to share the gospel and invest in another cultural setting. God burdened my Korean-American friend, Dan, to plant a church in a historically poor white neighborhood. God burdened my African-American friend, Marty, who grew up in the inner-city, to plant a church in the suburbs. God called a man named Paul, who wanted to work among his own people, to leave and take the gospel to the Gentiles. When God burdens a preacher for a people group, a neighborhood, or a block, it's right for that preacher to go and become all things to all people so that he might save some.

Reflecting on his own gospel work, the Apostle Paul wrote:

> For though I am free from all, I have made myself a servant to all, that I might win more of them. To the Jews I became as a Jew, in order to win Jews. To those under the law I became as one under the law (though not being myself under the law) that I might win those under the law. To those outside the law I became as one outside the law (not being outside the law of God but under the law of Christ) that I might win those outside the law. To the weak I became weak, that I might win the weak. I have become all things to all people, that by all means I might save some. I do it all for the sake of the gospel, that I may share with them in its blessings. (1 Cor. 9:19–23)

But you ask: *won't someone from the context have a better witness?*

Not necessarily. Don't misunderstand: God calls indigenous people to reach their fellows, but the gospel is "the power of God for salvation to everyone who believes" (Rom. 1:16). Additionally, the Apostle writes, "When I came to you, I did not come with eloquence or human wisdom as I proclaimed to you the testimony about God. For I resolved to know nothing while I was with you except Jesus Christ and him crucified" (1 Cor. 2:1–2).

What if God called Dan to the historically white neighborhood, and Marty to the suburban neighborhood, and myself to an African-American neighborhood so that "faith might not rest in the wisdom of men but in the power of God"? God may place the most unlikely vessel into a neighborhood so the only explanation for fruit might be God's supernatural work. Man cannot do this; only God can.

MOTIVES

However, fueled by biblical support, it's possible to rush into cross-cultural work without examining our *extra-biblical* motives. During my first few years, I was often questioned: "Why do *you* think you should plant a church here?" This initially took me by surprise as I had a lot to learn. But over time I realized that the question was a good one because it came from a place that was intimately familiar with the history of white superiority.

If you're eager to do cross-cultural ministry, here are a few questions you should be willing to ask yourself:

1. **Why am I here?** Are you here because of guilt, because you think you can save the day, or because you implicitly think you're way of doing life and church is superior?"
2. **Am I willing to submit to someone of a different ethnicity?** Do you have a mentor who's familiar with this context? If not, why not? Are you willing to find one? What might they say about your decision to plant a church here?
3. **Is there a need for a new church?** Are there other indigenous gospel works that you might consider joining? Should you submit to another pastor in this context? Are the other churches here actually unhealthy or are they merely operating from a different set of cultural values?

Essentially, you must ask yourself, ""Have I moved to this context unaware of the racial history and dynamics of the country and the community?"

LAND MINES

With those words of encouragement and examination, please allow me also offer a few potential land mines:

Land Mine #1: Trying to Be Someone You're Not

There's absolutely nothing worse than a white man who changes his dialect when talking to an African American. Marty tells me of his friend of 20 years who still tries to "talk jive" to him. "Becoming all things" doesn't mean you forget you're white and attempt to become another ethnicity. That's just annoying; it's also condescending. Remember your background and recognize any tensions your presence may arouse.

Land Mine #2: Imposing Your Own Culture On Other Ethnicities

You *do* have a culture. Your preaching style, liturgy, and hymns—including the way you sing them—are culturally influenced. Your cultural background has shaped your discipleship and ministry preferences. Your values, politics, and the way you talk about these things, are peppered with certain cultural standards.

Don't be like Peter in Galatians 2:11–14. Due to his fear and respect of leaders from his own culture, Peter breaks table fellowship with the Gentiles over cultural issues. Peter requires those who are ethnically different than him to assimilate in order to enjoy fellowship with him. Paul says "they were not acting in line with the truth of the gospel." The gospel doesn't allow anyone to set their cultural norms as the standard for discipleship.

Land Mine #3: Despising Those Who *Do* Look Like You

An unexpected temptation for many who are working in a cross-cultural context is a subtle disdain when members of their own ethnicity join their church. My friend, Dan, told me it took him a while to be okay with the fact that he still attracts other Korean-Americans to his church. You'll find people of your own hue attracted to your church because of you, and you've got to be okay with that. Don't make cross-cultural work an idol.

Land Mine #4: Drifting Toward Familiar Spaces

At the same time, there's another unexpected temptation,

and that's the draw toward familiarity. It's been said that the biggest missionary challenge is to *remain a missionary* once on the field. You will be drawn to socialize, mingle, and connect with those who look like you and are from the same background as you. This is natural. And yet, in order to remain a missionary, you must fight against these natural tendencies and intentionally develop cross-cultural friendships; learn to appreciate the values, pleasures, rhythms, and routines of your new neighbors. Sacrifice comfort and learn a new culture. Become all things to all people so that, by God's grace, you might win some.

CONCLUSION

I'm glad you want to serve a context different than your home culture. This demonstrates that God has torn down walls of ethnic division in your own life. As you carefully move forward in humility and with wisdom, be encouraged that God often uses cross-cultural work for his own glory.

ABOUT THE AUTHOR
Joel Kurz is the lead pastor of The Garden Church in Baltimore, Maryland. You can find him on Twitter at @joelkurz.

Church Planters, Don't Wait to Put Your Documents in Place

Joel Kurz

We waited three years to put our church documents in order, and we suffered for it.

We had a statement of faith—we needed one for funding—but we didn't know how to use it. No one ever encouraged us to adopt (and take seriously) a constitution or church covenant. Even if they did, I wouldn't have listened.

Church documents seemed outdated and rigid. I wanted to reach the people who these "other churches" weren't reaching. I wanted the people who didn't like the church, the people who were looking for something different.

Three years in, we put documents in place—and it was painful.

By that time, we'd attracted a group of people, many of whom disdained the local church. We knew that we were against legalistic and rigid churches, but we did not know what kind of church we wanted to become. Everything seemed up for discussion and debate, including the inerrancy of Scripture and substitutionary atonement. With no concept, or ability, to exercise church discipline, sin went unchecked. Challenges didn't work because everyone appealed to personal taste and would offer to "agree to disagree."

After three years of this, it was pretty clear that we were sinking. If Jesus' prayer was for unity in the church, his request didn't seem to be answered in ours.

Finally, we put a few documents in place. Our statement of faith took a prominent role in establishing what the church believed the Bible teaches. After many conversations and much research, we established a church constitution. We found a time-tested church covenant that simply outlined what the Bible requires of all believers.

And in the months to follow many people left, some angry, others frustrated.

So . . .

Church planters, don't wait three years to put some documents in place!

THE CHURCH IS A COUNTER-CULTURAL INSTITUTION

A restaurant may be organized a hundred different ways. The best of human wisdom can organize an excellent non-profit. But only Jesus can organize the local church. The Bible is where we find its organizing principles, and let me tell you: the church is *quite* the countercultural institution!

As you read the responsibilities that church members have for one another in passages like 1 Corinthians 5, or the leadership qualifications in 1 Timothy 3, you immediately get a profound sense that "flying by the seat of the pants" (as my mother would say) while organizing a new church just won't do. Without clear biblical guidelines, the new church plant may very well blend with pop-culture, and grow in less-than-helpful ways.

Theological Fuzziness

Drawing theological lines seems counterintuitive in our postmodern era. However, church plants don't naturally drift into orthodoxy. Not establishing doctrinal lines from the beginning causes the church to drift away from unity, integrity, and God's revealed truth. As a result, the budding church will likely be distracted by endless debates on core issues such as inerrancy and substitutionary atonement instead of engaging in what the planter *really* wants to engage in: mission!

Ecclesiological Squishiness

Who leads the church? Who is a church member and what's required of them? Who can serve in the church? Before our church organized, the diversity of answers we received to these questions was tremendous. Biblical church polity across the board is counter-cultural in society. Male eldership, congregational authority (for us Baptists), a baptized and regenerate church membership—these aren't ideas that we just come up with on our own. A church with no guiding principles on church government will likely guide themselves right out of biblical faithfulness.

Moral Ambiguity

What is required of a church member, and who determines this? A church plant, without documents, sets up their new flock for confusion. Can a cohabiting couple become members? Can a man living in clear, unrepentant sin serve in a public ministry? How do we handle a sister rebelling against Jesus?

Without clear biblical documents, church plants will drift toward legalism or licentiousness. Legalistically, they may place upon their members spiritual requirements that Jesus himself does not place upon them. Alternatively, their members may be given over to sin, having embraced an unchecked licentious lifestyle.

Because sinful people are called to plant and organize local churches, we need guiding principles that transcend human wisdom. We need biblical guidelines from the start.

THIS IS WHAT A CHURCH IS, AND WHO WE NEED TO BECOME

As a pastor, I often have the opportunity to counsel engaged couples. As part of our pre-marital counseling, I always explain in detail the expectations and requirements of marriage. Can you imagine someone getting married, and discovering the expectations and requirements of marriage three years later?

Lack of forethought and clarity as to *who* the church is, and *what* the church does, will lead to endless divisions. Responding to those divisions with documents (three years later) will feel reactionary and people will leave. Starting off with the documents will say from the get-go: *"This is what the church is, and this is what we need to become."*

Having documents at the beginning says: "We're a people of the Book."

Sometimes people ask, Isn't the Bible enough?

Well, in a sinless world, perhaps, we would all agree on what the Bible teaches. But in a fallen world various interpretations abound. Biblically saturated documents communicate that a church plant's vision is to be "built upon the foundation of the Apostles and Prophets" (Eph. 2:20).

By finally establishing documents, we were able to speak clearly to the people that God had given us, "This is what we believe the Bible says, and it's on this foundation that we stand. We not only recognize the need for biblical church leadership, but we spell it out. Ultimately, our documents detail and cast a vision for who we as a church will become. We not only admit that the Bible calls for pastoral integrity, but we formally place ourselves under the accountability of the church. These documents will provide you, church, protection from renegade, spineless, and authoritarian church planters. We not only discuss what membership looks like but we detail what God requires of the Christian—and what we, as a church, expect. These documents provide instant help when dealing with unrepentant sin and church discipline cases. They provide a vision of discipleship of each of our church plant team members, as well as new converts. We not only preach Galatians 1:6 (that we must not turn to another gospel), but we use these tools to articulate what that one, true gospel is. These documents serve to protect the church from false teachers and wolves."

TOOLS FOR DISCIPLESHIP

The Bible instructs churches to organize themselves in a way that flies in the face of current culture and fallen wisdom. Because of this, church plants need documents.

"We as a church grew significantly in spiritual health once we voted those (documents) in," said one member who's been with us since the beginning. It changed our church, and it changed our members. While some left, others responded positively, embraced the biblical vision, submitted themselves to the local church, and grew. Church planting is about making disciples, and documents are useful disciple-making tools.

ABOUT THE AUTHOR

Joel Kurz is the lead pastor of The Garden Church in Baltimore, Maryland. You can find him on Twitter at @joelkurz.

Planting Churches for Pleasure, Not for Profit

Nathan Knight

If you pay any attention to the land of church planting, you'll quickly begin to wonder if business mogul Jim Collins has taken control of its command center. Phrases like "customer-to-owner," "church launch," "preview services," and "entrepreneurial" have become ubiquitous, whereas those wonderfully powerful phrases we hear from Paul—"ambition to preach the gospel," "shepherd the flock of God among you," "preach the Word!"—seem to have been forgotten.

This is unfortunate, because what's needed to plant a church isn't the wisdom of Jim Collins, but the gospel of Jesus Christ and the word that testifies to that gospel. A cheap shot, I know, but listen—if we're going to enjoy the pleasure of God in planting a church, then we have to ignore whatever practices of men that promise to gather crowds quickly and instead mine the depths of God's Word in order to build a people intentionally.

Below I offer three principles we should all consider so that we might plant churches for the infinite pleasure of God's glory over and against our own profit.

BIBLE NOT BUSINESS

God's Word is sufficient, even for church planting. Whatever practices we need to give ourselves to are right there in the Bible, so long as we take the time to see them.

Discipleship, membership, preaching, discipline, elders, deacons, ordinances—all these things are spoken of plainly in the Bible. Each of them is a good gift from God that functions like a prong to fasten the church to the very same gospel she's called to proclaim and protect. In other words, things like membership and elders aren't just features we work into a plant after we've gathered a crowd; they're necessary ingredients that make up the compelling community that illustrates the character of God to a watching world.

The average church planting book gives little attention to describing and understanding what a church actually is. With good intentions, no doubt, these books often encourage church planters to prioritize profitability, such that "success" means getting as many people into the room as quickly as possible so they can attend your service. Usually, biblical markers for defining a church as a people—holy, set apart from the world—is at best a distant voice. Sometimes, it's not heard at all.

What is a church? Why does the church exist? What has God told us will mark his people? What should be taught? Who should lead? What should these leaders look like? What is success? The Bible has careful instructions on all of these things, which means it's more than sufficient to be our church planting guide.

PASTORS NOT PRESIDENTS

We may be familiar with Jesus' last words to his disciples, but what are the last words of that great church planter, the Apostle Paul? "Pay careful attention to yourselves and to all the flock, in which the Holy Spirit has made you overseers, to care for the church of God, which he obtained with his own blood" (Acts 20:28). Paul pleaded with these pastors to be shepherds who care, who love the flock that Jesus spilt his own blood to save.

Planters should not be entrepreneurs beginning a lemonade stand for Jesus. They should be pastors who gently handle the sheep of Christ and passionately push the glorious news of the gospel to places and people yet unnamed.

Visitors and church members should know we're not in it for a bigger platform. Instead, our lives should communicate our care for their souls. People can find magnetic and tantalizing personalities who are devoted to a specific good or service anywhere, but the church should offer something different. People are tired of being gamed for other people's profits. They want physicians who listen, honest car mechanics, politicians who get their hands dirty, and baristas who know their name. It's hard to find those kinds of leaders in the world, but people interested in the gospel should be able to find integrity in any leader of Christ's church.

Let's stop all these questions about being "entrepreneurial" and let's ask more questions about whether or not prospective planters love and care for their wives and their kids. Let's ask them about the last time they got a phone call late in the evening and they took it, gladly, because they wanted to serve those in trouble with the gospel. Let's ask planters if they'd be content with a little so that the Lord might entrust them with a lot.

RELATIONSHIPS NOT RIVALS

Before we chose to plant a church in Washington DC, not only did we talk to denominational leaders, we also—and more importantly—talked to godly people who actually lived here and were working. We did this for a few reasons.

First, we wanted to respect those who were already here. Secondly, in light of that, we wanted to hear from them if there were any gaps in the city that we could fill with a healthy, gospel-preaching church. We didn't want to preach the gospel where Christ had "already been named" (Rom. 15:20). Our lives are short, and the Lord has entrusted a lot to us. So we made it a priority to go to an underserved place, no matter whether or not it was a known or popular city. In fact, we actually had a couple other cities on our radar that we pulled away from because it seemed a lot of good work was going on there and it was going to be difficult to find a spot.

I see CVSs, Walgreens, and Rite Aides popping up everywhere—right on top of one another—in order to try and take the market share as rivals. Unfortunately, I sometimes notice the same thing happening among church planters.

Instead of building relationships, they listen only to their own camp, like a denominational leader who doesn't reside there but has "jurisdiction." Other church planters don't even ask questions about oversaturation because they assume every city is under-served and in need of their help.

But look at the Apostle Paul. One of his great joys was the fellowship he had with other churches. We miss out on that when we see others as rivals instead of family members to love, serve, and learn from.

Indeed, one of my greatest pleasures in church planting planting has been partnering together with a family of churches in the same city, "striving side by side for the faith of the gospel" (Phil. 1:27). We work together, not apart. The more we talk and listen to one another across denominational lines, the more the gospel fans out across the world, rather than pile up in one place.

ABOUT THE AUTHOR
Nathan Knight is the pastor of Restoration Church in Washington, D. C.

Knowing When to Say When: Reflections from a Failed Church Plant

Derek D. Bass

When I set out with my family to plant a church in Providence, Rhode Island writing on this topic of church planting failures never once crossed my mind. Instead, we'd envisioned reseeding Rhode Island and southern New England with gospel-driven churches—a line that still rings in my heart from some of our early material—and we'd prayed for our church to be first of many.

Planting a church in New England, and Providence in particular, wasn't something we did on a whim. I began discussing possibilities with Wes Pastor of The NETS Center for Church Planting & Revitalization while an unmarried doctoral student at Southern Seminary. The conversations continued as I married Elizabeth, continued my studies, and we had our first child. In July 2007, we moved from Louisville, Kentucky to Essex Junction, Vermont to enter into the 2-year residency program with NETS, which we extended another 2 years when I took a staff position at the church.

THE CHURCH PLANTING PROCESS

The process of planting a church from scratch was difficult and slow. We knew it would be tough, but I was perhaps more optimistic than realistic, thinking that it'd go a little faster for us.

We began by hosting Bible studies in our home. In the early days, just getting a few people around the living room was a smashing success; some weeks it was just Elizabeth, myself, and one or two neighbors. After two years of home Bible studies, marriage seminars, and numerous community outreach initiatives (Easter Egg hunts, a movie night in a local park, Bowling Night, a block party) we'd grown from our family of six to around 25 adults and children.

In September of 2013, we began monthly preview services in view of launching in January 2014. The services and the following months were both encouraging and discouraging. A husband and wife that Elizabeth and I had been investing in came to saving faith, but two other couples decided to depart the core team—the former in December and the latter in January. As long as it was taking to add people, these losses were devastating.

WHEN TO PULL THE PLUG

Answering the question, "How do you know when it's time to pull the plug on the plant?" is to me a bit like shepherding people through suffering. The moment of suffering isn't the time to introduce the reality of God's sovereignty. Rather, we should be *preparing* our people to suffer through consistent and thorough gospel-centered exposition from the whole Bible, building a gospel-centered worldview from which they'll rightly process life in a sin-filled world.

Similarly, church planting is hard work, and you need to set out with a support system. Because when it gets tough, you need to have brothers and sisters you can be real with. By God's grace, when we set out from

Burlington, Vermont to Providence, Rhode Island, we had a strong support system in place: 1) a sending church under whose authority we'd placed ourselves (and its leadership), 2) a mentor who'd been investing in us for four years, and 3) a network of church planters I could be honest with and call on in a time of need.

HOW WE KNEW

So, how did we know it was time?

First, I'd been struggling with whether pioneer church planting was my thing for over a year. In the previous two years I'd received two separate inquiries from schools wanting me to teach in their Old Testament department, one I quickly declined and the other I declined after a brief period of prayerful consideration. But by February 2014, I was beginning to wonder if I'd be more effective for the kingdom teaching or pastoring an existing church, rather than planting.

Second, I began to talk honestly with my wife concerning some of my own doubts.

Third, I was in frequent contact with my mentor, my older brother, who was a church planter in the Boston area, as well as a local pastor of another like-minded church (a re-plant) where we'd been worshipping until our church would launch. When a second couple left the plant in January, I was reaching out to these brothers for support and expressing my doubts. All were supportive, listened, asked questions, and offered encouragement. No one immediately recommended pulling the plug.

As I processed with these brothers, my wife, and a few others, some things stood out to me:

- The state of the church in Providence in 2014 was much better than in 2007, when we first considered moving and planting a church there.
- We were seeking to plant a church exactly one mile from a very like-minded church, which meant that when people moved to town looking for a church like ours, they'd typically end up there because it was already up and running. This was a big one for me.
- We didn't have any weight-bearing couples in our core team, so Elizabeth and I bore the majority of the weight.
- Whereas a year before, when offered a teaching position, I had no desire, now I felt free and at peace to move on from the plant with no job offer on the horizon. I was experiencing a change of desire.

This final point is clearly subjective, but it's directly related to the first two points; the freedom to move on from the plant was directly related to the changing state of things in Providence, and in particular my confidence in the leadership of certain churches. Without their faithful and fruitful efforts, I doubt I would have had such a peace.

Nevertheless, the decision to pull the plug on our plant was extremely difficult, gut-wrenching, and tearful. It left me wrestling through my identity in Christ. It felt like we'd experienced a death in the family.

And yet, as we moved forward, God, our good shepherd, kept his gracious hand upon us, led us into the green pastures of other pastoral ministries, and then opened the door for me to teach in Amsterdam at a missions seminary with over 20 nations represented in our student body. We're now missionaries in secular western Europe, helping to plant a church in Amsterdam and equipping students at Tyndale how to preach Christ rightly from the whole Bible by teaching them Hebrew Exegesis and Old Testament Theology. In this work, I'm regularly drawing on my difficulties and past church planting experience as I equip brothers to plant and pastor in some of the most strategic areas of the world.

Our God wastes absolutely nothing.

ABOUT THE AUTHOR
Derek Bass is an Assistant Professor of Old Testament Language and Literature at Tyndale Theological College in The Netherlands.

How to Merge Two Church Cultures

Dave Russell

A church merger brings together two groups that will inevitably have two different and pronounced cultures. The goal and the challenge in merging churches is to lead these two cultures to become one. In revitalization work, you're seeking to change a culture. In church planting, you're looking to build one. In a church merger, you must understand the two existing cultures and lead them to become one.

Here are five ways to do that.

1. CLARIFY THE EXPECTATIONS BEFORE YOU MERGE.

As in any relationship, before heading into a merger it's important to communicate the expectations that each group has. In the merger I recently led, one way we did this was by writing an "expectation document" that detailed what each group held important.

Here are the topics we covered:

- *What would a worship service look like?*
- *Do existing leaders in both groups expect positions when we merge?*
- *How would we approach existing church staff?*
- *How would the weekly schedule change?*

Through this conversation, we learned that the church we were merging with was concerned about their "home bound" members. This allowed us to put together a plan, before we merged, of how we'd minister to them together as one church. Rather than expecting me as the pastor to make every visit, we assigned members to take care of this important ministry.

Taking the time to discuss our expectations and document our agreements on the front end allowed us to purchase future peace.

2. TEACH THE BIBLE AS YOUR MOTIVATION AND EXPLANATION FOR CHANGE.

The church we merged with didn't have elders and had largely accepted the committee-driven approach to ministry. Our church, however, was committed to an elder-led and congregational approach. In our preliminary discussions, each group committed to studying the biblical offices of elder and deacon (1 Tim. 3:1–13). Gratefully, this study led to an agreement on our church constitution that proposed an elder-led and congregational church government.

While the leadership of both churches agreed on a number of issues, we needed to take the time to teach members of both groups. So we decided to have everyone go through a "Membership Class" together even before we merged. This gave us time to teach through both "what" would change and "why."

In addition to teaching through the Statement of Faith and Church Covenant, we spent a lot of time teaching through topics we knew people needed more exposure to. Specifically, we focused on church government and elders—where we see them in the Bible, what they are, what they aren't, how this looks in a Baptist church, how they'll be nominated and elected, etc. This allowed us to ground our reason for change in the Bible.

3. DON'T SHOCK THE SYSTEM—AND DON'T BE SHY.

When two churches merge, there's an expectation things will "reset." This expectation allows for certain changes early on. While it's certainly true that some leaders will struggle to be too ambitious and bring about too much change, others may be too reserved. Church mergers involve making decisions ahead of time that will help establish a new culture. Think carefully about changes that can be agreed upon that can set up future success.

The biggest change I went for before the merge was to the move to an elder-led church. While most revitalization work would move slowly toward this, our merger provided the opportunity to set this up quickly. Thankfully, this transition set our church up for fruitfulness. In fact, there's no question in my mind that things wouldn't have gone nearly as well if we'd held off. Lead with gentleness and patience—but also lead with shrewdness, discerning the changes that you can move quickly on.

4. THERE IS NO "US" AND "THEM."

The night we officially merged we had all of our members come together for a "Covenant Service" where we signed the Statement of Faith and Church Covenant. After taking time to sing and listen to a message, we took the Lord's Supper. At this moment, our two groups became one. From that point forward, we communicated that we never wanted there to be an "us" and "them." A new group had been formed, and we were now one church.

The first commitment listed in our Church Covenant quotes from Ephesians 4:3, that we'd be "eager to maintain the unity of the Spirit in the bond of peace." Our merger brought a unity that each member is called to guard and preserve. While there would certainly be a period of transition and some awkwardness in adjusting, we needed to be guided by Scripture in maintaining the unity of one body.

5. COMMIT TO SHOWING HONOR TO ONE ANOTHER.

In most mergers, one church is declining and another is growing. That was true in our case. The group that came from the declining church had experienced some sadness; their ministry had declined over the years. However, the group from our growing church came in with momentum and joy. Some had been laboring in the same church for decades (as many as 60 years!), while others had been meeting only for a matter of months. One group was older, the other was younger.

In the midst of all this, the leadership and members needed to commit to "outdo one another in showing honor" (Rom. 14:10).

Merging two churches requires a commitment to honor one another by speaking well of one another, by building relationships across the barriers of culture and age, and by broadly showing brotherly affection in the church.

In our situation, I wanted to be careful to honor the history of the church. So, when we marked our one-year replant anniversary, three months later we threw a big celebration for the 80th anniversary of the church that existed before we merged. We celebrated the present and honored the past because together we had a new future. "Their" history had become "our" history because two had become one.

ABOUT THE AUTHOR

Dave Russell is a pastor at Oakhurst Baptist Church in Charlotte, North Carolina. You can find him on Twitter at @DRussinDC.

Church Mergers and Tolerable Irregularities

Brad Wheeler

About a week ago I was meeting with a member who desired to be married. I asked him about his "list," that spreadsheet of "non-negotiables" he values in any woman who would be his spouse. And without missing a beat he somewhat playfully retorted, "I really only have one. *I don't do ugly*." In his relational "triage," beauty was the non-negotiable.

Leaving aside the wisdom (or utter lack thereof!) of his response, when it comes to whether or not a man should pastor a church, we have to do our own triage. We have our own lists of those things that are non-negotiables, those matters that are strong-preferences, and those that are truly indifferent. These issues arise inevitably and immediately as one church considers merging with another, though they also have more general relevance for men who are considering a pastorate.

But how do we decide which matters fall into which buckets? Granting at least some level of theological and methodological difference, when should two churches merge despite the differences—and when should they stay separate precisely because of the differences?

FIRST, DO YOUR HOMEWORK.

You can't make quality judgments without quality information. Just because a church is willing to hire you, doesn't mean you should be willing to pastor her. During the housing bubble, NINJA (no income, no job, no asset) loans were all the rage. Yet they came with a catch. The rate often started low. It looked immediately attractive. But then over time it starts to kick-up, and you pay for it on the back-end. Sadly, many homeowners who were suckered into such loans were left bankrupt and on the street.

Similarly, a pastor shouldn't assume. He must do his homework. He ought to look at a church's governing documents such as their statement of faith, church covenant (if they have one), and constitution or by-laws. He ought to ask for a detailed copy of the church's budget. For just as a personal budget reflects one's priorities, so a church's budget reflects the spiritual priorities of that body and will tell you much about what she values. He ought to meet with leaders, learn about the church's history, gather information about its strengths and weaknesses. While churches don't tend to be intentionally deceptive, what immediately looks attractive could be hiding something that will leave you on the street a few years later.

SECOND, KNOW YOURSELF.

What risks can you reasonably take? Younger men who are single can likely take more risks than married men with four kids entering high school. For though the church only calls the man, that ministry will affect the whole family. And transitions, especially on children, tend to become harder the older they are. If you're married, know your wife and her season of life. What can she reasonably bear? Part of living with your wife "in an understanding way" ought to consider her with the utmost care.

Know yourself, and know your own strengths and weaknesses and how they'll play to the church's culture. Similarly, are you doing it alone, or will you have a "wingman" beside you? Every Maverick ought to have a Goose. It's different if you have someone who has your back, complements your weaknesses, and loves you enough to press in and challenge you, and yet will support and encourage you as you fight the good fight together. The more difficult the church's situation, the more critical it is that you're not going at it alone.

THIRD, KEEP THE MAIN THINGS IN VIEW.

With respect to a church, the pulpit is like the rudder of a ship. Without it, you can't change direction, and you shouldn't even try. In other words, I don't recommend trying to do any kind of significant "reform" or "revitalization" work unless you have the pulpit to help set the course of the church's agenda along the Bible's agenda. If you have the pulpit, there's probably very little, if anything, that you must *immediately* change.

Beyond the pulpit, it's necessary to be in agreement *on those things essential for salvation*. Did Jesus bodily rise from the grave? Must one repent and believe in order to be saved? This is part of what marks a church as a "true" church over a "false" church. If there's not clear agreement on such evangelical basics, then there's little common foundation to build upon.

This doesn't mean you're certain every member will be saved (only the Lord knows the heart), or even clear on those beliefs essential for salvation. Some churches are poorly taught, and thus are comprised of a plethora of disparate beliefs and practices. Yet if the governing documents are clear in their evangelical conviction, and there's at least some support within the congregation for those beliefs, you have a foundation to begin your work. But if the church, either through their governing documents and/or explicit teaching and history *clearly* disagrees with the basics of evangelical conviction, it's likely not kind to them (or you!), and it will be unnecessary to pick a fight. Related to this would be the church's conviction about the Bible.

While it's necessary to agree on those things essential for salvation, it's also wise to be in agreement *on those secondary matters essential for gathering together*. This is where you have a true church, but it may be irregular in some of its practices. This is where items like baptism and ecclesiology come into play. If you think you can get a baby wet but can't baptize it, it's not wise to take a church that will require you to violate your conscience. Nor is it likely wise or kind of you to come in quietly, but with the clear intent to *change* their practice. If they established themselves as a paedobaptist church, and practice paedobaptism because that's what they clearly believe the Bible to teach, it's foolish if not cruel to take the pastorate with the intent to make them something else. Simply find another credobaptist church, and let them continue in their ministry with a paedobaptist pastor.

When it comes to polity, like baptism, every church practices one form or another, if they don't realize it. Now churches don't tend to adhere to their polity with the same rigor as baptism, so perhaps there's more wiggle-room here. As a congregationalist, I would be deeply hesitant to take a church where the authority is understood to be in a bishop from another city or state, or a presbytery from another collection of churches. Churches where the authority lies finally within the congregation's elders is certainly better, for at least the authority lies with members of that local church. And in practice, many elder-rule churches meaningfully incorporate the congregation into their decision-making. So while they may be irregular in their understanding of polity, in practice it may look more regular.

Two other convictions may similarly fall into this category. The first would be inerrancy. For while a belief in inerrancy isn't necessary for salvation, pastors will preach as if the Bible is true or not. And if the congregation isn't willing to recognize the authority of the Scriptures in faith and practice, it will make your job difficult if not impossible. A second would be the ability of the congregation to congregate together. If you believe a church is a gathered congregation, than having a facility that can seat everyone will be critically important.

There are many other matters one can simply locate on the spectrum of *preference to indifference*. Where is the church located (metropolitan/suburban/rural, Northeast or Southwest)? Many treat this as a first-order issue (think "I don't do ugly"). But in my mind, while it's not unimportant, it should be well down the list. Coming from Northern California, I never imagined landing in Arkansas. But the church I now have the privilege of pastoring shared my convictions on those things essential for salvation and essential for gathering together. And that has made my job an incredible joy.

Here are other important questions: do they have elders? Deacons? Do they have a building? Is there a lot of debt? What's the church's size? Obviously some of those matters are more important than others. But none of those matters alone would necessarily steer me away from serving a church.

So, as you think about pastoring a church, or advising others on the pastorate of a church, consider carefully your own triage. And make sure you're reasoning with a biblical lens, and not simply a worldly one.

ABOUT THE AUTHOR
Brad Wheeler is the senior pastor of University Baptist Church in Fayetteville, Arkansas.

Anatomy of a Church Merger

John Folmar

Once upon a time there was a young, vibrant church in Louisville with sound doctrine, superb teaching, and warm fellowship—it was Trinity Baptist Church, pastored by Tom Schreiner, Shawn Wright, and others.

A great church—but they had no building and weren't as rooted in the community as they wanted to be. Church members were transient, mostly students connected to the nearby Southern Baptist Theological Seminary.

At the same time there was an older congregation in the Clifton neighborhood of Louisville that had a great heritage, a beautiful building, and a solid connection to the community. But the ministry was dwindling, down to maybe 70 people—most in their 70s—with little emphasis on expository ministry, and little evangelistic outreach.

My family and I arrived at Clifton in 2000 and loved it immediately, recognizing the potential for reform. I'll never forget Gene, regularly at the door handing lollipops to our daughter; or Amby, dutifully serving in the nursery (with only our kids enrolled). We grew to love these saints but, at the same time, we grieved because the Word was not being preached. The sermons consisted only of stories and anecdotes. The gospel was largely assumed.

WHAT IF?

I remember thinking: what if we took the strengths of Trinity and combined them with the strengths of Clifton—and formed one united church? Why not couple the energy and doctrinal fidelity of the one with the building and heritage of the other?

I proposed the idea, but the leadership of Clifton summarily dismissed it. They were looking for their own pastor, and some of them—not all—were opposed to Southern Seminary and the guiding theology of Trinity Baptist. I still remember some of the old search committee poring over Tom Schreiner's Romans commentary (which I had given them) and objecting to some of his views.

The proposal was dead in the water. No way would it work. But some of us just kept praying about it. And the Lord began slowly moving people off of that search committee. Some left the church, disgruntled. Others moved away. And eventually, to my amazement, they asked me to chair the search committee! But it remained a very delicate situation.

Once again, I proposed the merger of Trinity and Clifton. I'll never forget the first time Tom met with the other members of the search committee—and they loved him! I was struck by how candid and open Tom was in his dealings with them. Here was a man who really loved these people, really wanted the merger to happen, and yet would not shade the truth at all in order to win their support. Whether it was issues of theology or ministry philosophy, he just laid all his cards on the table, told them what he thought, and gave them reasons why. He was wise in addressing potential differences, but he was not deceptive.

Then came the day when Tom preached at Clifton with a view to a call and brought about a hundred of Trinity's members. It was an unsettling time for Clifton—their identity and their church were in many ways threatened—but in God's kindness it was a joyous joining together of two different communities for the glory of God, and the rest is history.

FOUR LESSONS

Here are four lessons that I learned from our church merger.

1. God is sovereign over the affairs of local churches.

Watching how the Lord removed opposition to the merger and changed people's hearts toward Trinity was one of the most amazing demonstrations of God's sovereignty I've ever encountered. It was like night and day—from settled opposition to almost unanimous approval. God had changed people's hearts.

2. There will inevitably be fallout.

Some disgruntled Clifton members departed immediately, others wandered away over time. But others stayed, and their lives were changed forever. Some of them were converted. One particularly painful departure was the music minister. He'd been an enthusiastic proponent of the merger from the beginning because he longed for revival. He was a good-hearted brother but, in terms of ministry philosophy and theology, he was on a different page. Eventually he left. It was a painful, but not ungodly, parting.

3. Trust in the Lord with all your heart and lean not on your own understanding.

I'll never forget the way Tom Schreiner and some of the other leaders obviously trusted the Lord in the whole thing. On the Clifton side of things, I so badly wanted this to happen that I was prone to work, scheme, fret, be political, and form alliances—but Tom just showed up and straightforwardly, openly stated the way he expected things to move forward if the merger happened. I learned a lot about trusting God through observing Trinity's leadership and transparency those days.

4. Genuine believers love one another.

There were a million ways this could have gone wrong. The two congregations were as different as you can possibly imagine—culturally, musically, theologically, everything. And yet, Trinity came in and didn't take things over, but rather patiently built their lives into the lives of the Clifton congregation. And Clifton didn't resist the newcomers as they might have been tempted to, but rather welcomed them with open arms.

These saints—from so many different walks of life, different backgrounds, and different generations—genuinely grew to love each other, bear with each other, and serve each other.

It was one of the greatest things I've ever had the privilege of witnessing: the reform of a local church, for the glory of God, almost overnight.

ABOUT THE AUTHOR

John Folmar is the pastor of United Christian Church of Dubai in the United Arab Emirates.

What I Learned from Two Failed Church Mergers

Matthew Cunningham

ACT ONE: A NEARBY SBC BAPTIST CHURCH

Sometimes I take walks with people instead of meeting them for lunch or at the office. I guess Steve Jobs biography inspired me. He closed some of Apple's biggest deals walking barefoot around Palo Alto with billionaire executives.

One day, I was walking with one of our elders, talking and praying about finding a church building. At this point, our church was about four years old and meeting in a middle school cafeteria with no windows, but a few "Got Milk" posters with Miley Cyrus.

As we were walking, it suddenly struck us that there was a big, almost-empty Baptist church nearby. So we walked over and knocked on the door. We were greeted by a group of older gentlemen playing dominoes in the fellowship hall. These men had been members of the church for decades. A few years prior, the church had lost its pastor to moral failure, and they were down to about 20 people in attendance on Sunday mornings. This once-thriving congregation had a building that sat 500 and dozens of unused classrooms.

Over time, a conversation about merging our two congregations began. After a few meetings with their leadership team, they were ready to bring the merge to a congregational vote. We were naive and ecstatic. On the evening of the vote, I received a call from the chairman of the deacons informing me that the congregation had voted the merger down. I was caught off-guard.

"There must be something we can do," I said.

"Nope," he replied, "the congregation has voted, and that's it."

"But I thought that everyone was on board," I said.

"Well, our membership roster has hundreds of people that don't attend the church. They showed up for the business meeting and voted the idea down. End of story," he said.

LESSONS LEARNED FROM FAILURE #1

1. **Go slowly and build relationships.** The time between the first conversations and the vote was only about 6 weeks. It simply wasn't long enough for the churches to get to know each other. In my estimation, it takes 3 to 12 months to learn enough about a church to make a decision to merge.
2. **Ask questions about the membership and polity.** Many of the questions that you think you should ask, you'll likely already ask—determining if they're a congregational church, asking about the elders' authority, etc. But you should also ask more detailed questions about the expectations of membership. Ask about what they mean by congregationalism. Ask

about what typical members' meetings look like. Ask how many people attend members' meetings.

3. **Lead and pastor before you're the leader and pastor.** This church was being held hostage by a contingency of people that never attended the church. These people were not in covenant relationship with the congregation. They were people who viewed the church as some kind of legacy, or social club, or vestige of the past that was theirs to preserve. The church needed us to lead them through the process of some level of meaningful membership prior to bringing the merger to a vote.

4. **Ask for outside help.** It's hard and awkward to have blunt and loving conversations. We were aware of some of the un-health in the church, but didn't feel it was really our place to address the issues. At least, it seemed too self-serving for us to address the things we saw, so we decided to let the issues go and planned to address them after the merge. This obviously never happened.

ACT TWO: A NEARBY BGC BAPTIST CHURCH

I was sitting in my study when my phone rang; it was another elder in the church. He informed me that he was having coffee with a pastor from a nearby church and that I should join him because I'd want to hear what he had to say.

When I arrived, this pastor said he'd like us to consider merging as one local church. They were a historic congregation that owned a facility on one of the busiest streets on this side of town. They had experienced decline, but were still a faithful congregation. Their pastor was a good Bible teacher and was looking for help to see his congregation thrive again.

This time around, we decided to go slower than we did the first time—and each congregation's elders asked a third-party mediator to advise and mentor throughout the process.

I also received advice from some pastors that were part of an aggressive church planting network. They advised me that we needed to "have a funeral" for the other church, and that it "needed to die," and that "if that pastor has failed, he needs to get out of the way."

Unfortunately, my own arrogance led to the breakdown of the conversation. The members at the other church wanted to ensure that their pastor had a paid position for a season but I made it clear this was not an option. This effectually ended the conversation. The two churches never took the matter to a vote.

LESSONS LEARNED FROM FAILURE #2:

1. **Look to reestablish a gospel witness in the neighborhood.** Some of the advice I was receiving was to see the church die and have a funeral. A better approach would have been to see a gospel witness restored to the area. One of the ways you may end up serving another local church is by actually not merging, but instead seeing them enter into a new season of fruitfulness. Thankfully, this church was able to do this on their own. The pastor stayed, the congregation remained intact, and the church began to thrive again. Even though things ended a little abruptly in our merger talks, they were able to glean a lot from watching us for a season and from the coaching of the outside counsel we each were receiving.

2. **Be gracious and considerate to the current leadership team.** This church had men, and particularly one man (the pastor), who were faithfully seeking to shepherd their church to new pastures of health. It was an incredible act of humility for him even to approach us and ask us to consider merging with them. We should have honored these brothers for their faithfulness, commended them for their leadership, and encouraged the church to respect their authority. If these men are qualified, be

open to their leadership as elders after the merger.

3. **Initial excitement, questionable impressions, and, finally, relationships.** There is always an initial excitement about a new opportunity, but this is just the honeymoon phase. Then come questionable impressions about motives, actions, behaviors, etc. This is a tough stage to get past—this second time, we didn't make it. We were still too much about business and "getting the job done." I wish we'd realized the end game is real relationships. I wish we'd spent more time working to break down false impressions. Just like most of the significant things in our lives, there are no shortcuts in church mergers; they require time, patience, and faithfulness.

Currently, we're approaching a third potential merger opportunity. Hopefully, I won't need to write "More Lesson Learned" next year.

ABOUT THE AUTHOR
Matthew Cunningham is the lead pastor of The Gathering Church in Portland, Oregon.

When Two Become One

Jonathan Rourke

A merger between churches is like a marriage between people. Two independent entities come together under a unifying covenant and witnesses. Though the union is ultimately spiritual, there are still legal issues that have to be settled before the two become one in the eyes of the state. This article outlines the legal considerations of a church merger. It's not a recipe for the success of the marriage, but a roadmap for blending families. It's not very romantic, but it's necessary.

First comes love, then comes contracts, then comes marriage.

MEMORANDUM OF UNDERSTANDING

Once the preliminary discussions about the intent to merge have happened, the paperwork begins. The first document you need to draft is the **Memorandum of Understanding**. This is your "just so we're clear on everything" document. It will guide you though the whole merger process and protect both parties from misunderstandings that can take you off course and compromise your reputation. Think of it as the somewhat awkward DTR (define the relationship) conversation you have after a couple dates. This document does not require a lawyer, but should include the following sections.

1. A few paragraphs outlining the **history** of how both churches arrived at this point. It helps to give an honest description of the factors that led to the decision. In the early years, it's common for the stronger church to be accused of a hostile takeover. The best answer is to produce the record of why merging was considered a good thing for everyone involved.
2. A statement of **purpose** follows, detailing how the process and details of the merger would be adopted by each congregation. Since the bylaws and practices usually differ, it's essential to clarify how *each church* will execute the terms of the agreement should the merger be completed.
3. An overview of the **process** should be included to clarify each step along the way. This includes where the new church will be physically located, what staff changes will occur, what votes and thresholds will be required, and how the transfer of church membership, property, assets, and liabilities will take place. It's helpful to propose a timeline beginning with the approval of the memorandum of understanding, and concluding with the first joint service as a merged body.
4. The specific **entity** is described next, namely which corporation will remain, which will dissolve, and what will happen to the assets of the dissolving entity. It's also important to make sure the officers of

the surviving corporation are made up of people the new church approves. Contact the secretary of state for the legal (and fictitious) name(s) of both corporations. These change sometimes and don't always reflect the name on the sign out front. Often, an amendment to the articles of incorporation has been filed with the secretary of state, and the name is legally changed. Identify the officers of each corporation, usually a President/CEO, Secretary, and Treasurer. State law dictates how this is registered and recorded, but if officers are no longer at the church, it's imperative to sort this out prior to the merger.

5. The next section contains the proposed **personnel** structure, including the names and positions of all staff members who will be serving the new church. This will usually include at least the following positions: Senior Pastor, Associate Pastor(s), and Bookkeeper/Office Personnel.

6. **Governance** is also an important consideration, so this section should be clear. In short, it should describe the polity of the new church. Upon completion of the merger, the Constitution and Bylaws of the surviving entity will be in force. If the leadership of the surviving entity will not be retained in full, or augmented with others, then this needs to be spelled out in detail. There needs to be a clear explanation of who will comprise the new governing body, and when this will take effect.

7. **Accounting** considerations are mentioned next. It should be clear that the new church will own all assets and liabilities. Furthermore, the paragraph should contain information regarding the fiscal year, the need for an annual review or audit of the financials, and a commitment to maintaining Generally Accepted Accounting Principles (GAAP). Finally, the document should outline an allocation of costs associated with the merger. These will likely be shared by the churches and involve the cost of consulting, legal, and accounting services. There will also be an assortment of filing fees and banking expenses.

8. **Ministries** in both churches will be affected by the merge. A paragraph about which ones will continue, be added, or be removed is essential. Missionaries or other non-profits currently being supported by either church need to be given notice if their funding will change, and it should be clearly spelled out who will be included in the new church budget.

9. One last consideration is **dissolution**. Certainly no one plans on the merger failing, but that doesn't mean it's risk-free. With all the prayer, meetings, effort, and money involved, proper stewardship demands a clear strategy if the endeavor collapses. This includes what will happen regarding employee severance, real property, and assets. It should also stipulate what conditions would be placed on the sale of the property.

AGREEMENT OF MERGER

Once the **Memorandum of Understanding** has been signed by the governing body of each church, an **Agreement of Merger** can be drafted for the whole congregation to approve. It's important to remember that if you're a church, you're a corporation. In the eyes of the state, a church is simply a non-profit corporation with all the benefits and obligation that come with that.

The **Agreement of Merger** is what will be approved or rejected by the church. Except in rare cases, most corporate bylaws related to churches require some kind of congregational vote to approve a merger, accusation, or dissolution of the corporation. So this document is what the two churches will use as the terms and conditions of their new relationship. It's like a prenuptial agreement intended to protect each other in the unlikely event of a breakup.

This legal document is usually drafted by a lawyer and based off the memorandum of understanding. It's the legal document that will be filed with the Secretary of State in compliance with individual state law, along with the document mentioned below.

CERTIFICATE OF APPROVAL OF AGREEMENT OF MERGER

Assuming the measure passes, attached to the **Agreement of Merger** will be a **Certificate of Approval of Agreement of Merger** for *each* church. This is a one-page document, signed by the officers of the corporation, that certifies each congregation voted in favor of the merger. It explains that on a certain date the **Agreement of Merger** was finalized, approved by the governing board, and then approved by the congregation in keeping with the Constitution and bylaws of each church. It should show that there is only one class of voting member, and the total number of eligible members. It should also mention that the Attorney General is not required to consent to the merger if that's the case in your state.

CERTIFICATE OF CORPORATE VOTE

When the time comes for each church's membership to vote on the merger, a special meeting should be called in which a ballot containing all the general conditions of the merger is presented for a vote. After it's been completed, a **Certificate of Corporate Vote** is produced. This document, to be completed within 90 days of the vote, certifies that the vote took place at a certain place and time, a quorum of members was present, and the measure was approved by a margin in keeping with the bylaws of the church. It is signed and dated by the Secretary/Clerk of the corporation. It ultimately functions as a record for the church so it's not submitted to the Secretary of State.

HOW LONG WILL IT TAKE?

The steps outlined here don't need to take a long time to execute. In the merger I was a part of, both elder boards approved the memorandum of understanding, an agreement of merger was drafted by an attorney, both congregations voted on the merge, paperwork was certified by the Secretary of State, staff transitions occurred, a new elder board was established, and the first joint service was held—all within six weeks.

That may sound like a shotgun wedding, but it isn't. When all the particulars of the merger are out in the open and on paper, the interested parties can arrive at a conclusion with relative ease. It will also provide answers to opponents who may surface in the weeks or years following the merger.

ABOUT THE AUTHOR
Jonathan Rourke is the senior pastor of Tri-City Bible Church in Vista, California. You can follow him on Twitter at @JonathanRourke.

Made in the USA
Monee, IL
14 November 2019